HOT Skills:

Developing Higher-Order Thinking in Young Learners

Other Redleaf Press books by Steffen Saifer

Practical Solutions to Practically Every Problem: The Survival Guide for Early Childhood Professionals, Third Edition

HOT Skills

DEVELOPING HIGHER-ORDER THINKING IN YOUNG LEARNERS

Steffen Saifer, EdD

Redleaf Press®
www.redleafpress.org
800-423-8309

Published by Redleaf Press
10 Yorkton Court
St. Paul, MN 55117
www.redleafpress.org

First edition 2018
Cover design by Tom Heffron
Cover photograph and illustration by iStock.com/ideabug and iStock.com/bulentgultek
Interior design by Michelle Lee Lagerroos
Typeset in Arno Pro, DIN 2014, and Black Coffee
Interior photos and illustrations: Art images on page 27, clockwise: Rosenwald Collection, courtesy of the National Gallery of Art; Gift of the W. L. and May T. Mellon Foundation, courtesy of the National Gallery of Art; Collection of Mr. and Mrs. John Hay Whitney, courtesy of the National Gallery of Art; Chester Dale Collection, courtesy of the National Gallery of Art; Chester Dale Collection, courtesy of the National Gallery of Art; Gift of Mrs. John D. Rockefeller 3rd, in Honor of the 50th Anniversary of the National Gallery of Art, courtesy of the National Gallery of Art; Collection of Mr. and Mrs. Paul Mellon, courtesy of the National Gallery of Art; Collection of Mr. and Mrs. Paul Mellon, courtesy of the National Gallery of Art; tree images on page 30–31, L-R: iStock.com/nancykennedy, iStock.com/AVTG, iStock.com/Whiteway, iStock.com/weible1980, iStock.com/mirceax, iStock.com/jdt01fgo, iStock.com/heliopix, iStock.com/Jill_InspiredByDesign, iStock.com/anmbph, iStock.com/alphavisions, iStock.com/CribbVisuals, iStock.com/FrankvandenBergh; Page 51: iStock.com/Alex Belomlinsky, iStock.com/webeedesign, iStock.com/Vectorchoice; Page 53: iStock.com/Steve Debenport, iStock.com/WilleeCole, iStock.com/isaravut, iStock.com/olaser; Page 151: iStock.com/Victor_85, iStock.com/FrankRamspott, iStock.com/Денис Калетник, iStock.com/Serhii Brovko, iStock.com/chokkicx, iStock.com/Sergey Oplanchuk, iStock.com/RedKoalaDesign, iStock.com/skalapendra; Page 152: iStock.com/pijama61, iStock.com/AVIcons

Printed in the United States of America
25 24 23 22 21 20 19 18   1 2 3 4 5 6 7 8

Library of Congress Cataloging-in-Publication Data
CIP Data has been applied for.

Printed on acid-free paper

To my children and their children and the generations to come.
May they learn from my generation's mistakes to be

more kind than we have been heartless,

more responsible than we have been puerile,

more respectful than we have been churlish,

more generous than we have been mercenary,

more honest than we have been venal,

more erudite than we have been foolish,

more peaceful than we have been savage.

Contents

Chapter 9: HOT Techniques for HOT Teaching: Intentional *and* Playful

Chapter 10: Teaching Reading and Writing Using Higher-Order Thinking: Yearning to Learn

Table of Figures

Acknowledgments

I am beholden to the dozens of thought leaders whose wisdom has inspired me over the course of my career. Some are friends and colleagues, some are acquaintances, and some I know only through their higher-order thinking: Elena Bodrova, Barbara Bowman, Alicia Brandwine, Berry Brazelton, Sue Bredekamp, Nancy Carlsson-Paige, Margie Carter, Deb Curtis, Linda Darling-Hammond, Stanislas Dehaene, Daniel Dennett, Stephanie Feeney, Michael Fullan, Howard Gardner, Dan Gartrell, Stacie Goffin, Janet Gonzalez-Mena, Jim Greenman, Vivian Gussin Paley, James Hymes, Marilou Hyson, Elizabeth Jones, Daniel Kahneman, Lilian Katz, Herb Kohl, Jonathan Kozol, Cassie Landers, Deborah Leong, Eda LeShan, Rebecca Marcon, Sam Meisels, A. S. Neill, Robert Pianta, Daniel Pink, Steven Pinker, Jack Shonkoff, Daniel J. Siegel, Dorothy Singer, Jerome Singer, James Wertsch, Martin Woodhead, and Ed Zigler.

Introduction

Nothing makes me happier and more hopeful than seeing great teachers work their magic. Like most people, I intuitively know a great teacher when I see one, but describing exactly what makes a teacher great is not so easy. Although I can readily see the results of their magic—students are engaged, excited, motivated, inquisitive, happy, productive, and learning—it has taken me quite a while to figure out just *how* they do it. As it turns out, how they do it is not readily observable and, as with magic tricks, what *is* observable can obscure the actions that create the magic. Great teachers, like magicians, often do two or more things at the same time. Here are two examples:

- I observed a teacher helping a group of kindergartners resolve a conflict about how to build a castle with blocks. She only asked questions and stayed with them until they came up with their own solutions. "What does everyone think of Ray's idea?" "Does someone have another idea?" "What task can Sam do that would help the group?" "Why does that feel unfair to you?" "What would make it more fair?" "Does everyone agree?" The students had surprisingly sophisticated ideas and negotiation skills. They ended up with an agreement to build several different versions of the castle.

- A second-grade teacher, whose students were all children or grandchildren of farmworkers, created a theme-based study of local crops, farming, and farm work. Lessons based on state standards in math, science, social studies, reading, writing, and art were integrated into the activities. In addition, the students learned how wages and prices are set and a few other basic economic concepts. Among other activities, students interviewed family members and wrote their stories in English and Spanish, with photos and drawings. The class created a board game called From Farm to Table that tracks crops from planting to consuming and presents obstacles like drought, overplanting, shortage of workers, striking truckers, negotiations with retailers, competition, marketing costs, and changing food preferences of consumers. The teacher created a website with the students' work, which they proudly shared with their families on cell phones or on computers in the community library.

In the first example, the teacher asked questions that required higher-order thinking to answer. The teacher knew she could ask difficult, abstract questions and the students would rise to the challenge because the questions were carefully worded to promote social harmony, something very important to these kindergartners. While overtly helping students resolve a conflict, she also taught conflict resolution skills, fostered positive relationships, and promoted higher-order thinking. This engaged both their intellect and their emotions.

In the second example, the teacher gave his students challenging work requiring a range of higher-order thinking. He taught them grade-level content as well as abstract concepts beyond the expectations of typical second graders, particularly for students whose family language is not English. They were able to rise to these challenges because the teacher considered their cultural values and personal lives. Family members, family life, and relationships were very important to these Latino children. All the lessons were based in a context that was understandable and meaningful to them.

Great teachers fully engage students by challenging them intellectually while making learning enjoyable and meaningful, and by providing emotional support. They compel their students to use a wide variety of higher-order thinking skills at increasingly advanced levels many times every day.

I wrote this book to help all teachers do what great teachers do. For several reasons, I focused on the aspect of great teaching that engages students' higher-order thinking. I had already coauthored a book on cultural responsive teaching

(Saifer et al. 2011), and there are many other excellent books on this topic. From my observations and reviews of research, I've found teaching strategies that engage students' higher-order thinking are rare, although they are not necessarily more difficult or time-consuming than other teaching strategies. I focused on young learners because it is important to start developing higher-order thinking skills early. Even very young children are capable of using many types of higher-order thinking (HOT) skills at surprisingly advanced levels when given opportunities, support, guidance, and practice. Developing students' higher-order thinking is a powerful strategy for improving educational outcomes for all students, and I explain why I believe this later in the book. I also give many examples and detailed descriptions of how developing HOT skills can be done in ways that are developmentally appropriate, engaging, challenging, and enjoyable.

Why do we so rarely see teachers of young learners promote HOT skills? I believe there are five main reasons:

1. Many teachers do not realize that very young students are capable of higher-order thinking.

2. Teachers were not taught this way when they were young, nor did they learn to teach HOT skills in their teacher training courses.

3. Rather than developing children's thinking skills, teachers view their work as informing young students, ensuring that they have basic school readiness skills and are well prepared for the curriculum in the next grade.

4. Most curricula teachers are given to use, and the associated tests, do not require—or even lend themselves to—using higher-order thinking skills.

5. Supervisors' expectations for how teachers should teach and the criteria used to evaluate them do not include promoting higher-order thinking skills.

I am, however, very hopeful that things can and will change. Whenever I suggest ideas to teachers for promoting HOT skills, they are always very excited and anxious to try them out. In one such incident in the Gambia (West Africa), I observed an activity designed to teach (or perhaps reinforce) colors to four- and five-year-old students. While each child flipped through a small board book, the teacher asked, "What color is this?" for each page. Later, during snacktime, when he asked me for feedback, I suggested that he could ask the students to think of a color that was not in the book. His eyes brightened, but he didn't say anything. To my delight, right after snack, he asked his students this question, although he had planned a different activity. It was a completely new type of question for the students, so, not surprisingly, he got no response. He reviewed the colors that were in the book and asked again, and again he got no response. He then took the students outside, as the outer walls of the building were colorfully painted and the plants, flowers, and trees provided even more colors to see. But the students were still unable to name other colors. He finally had to point out to the students some colors that were not in the book.

Some teachers would conclude that this question is too difficult for young students. Some would say that it is developmentally inappropriate for four-year-olds. But most of these students had never been asked this type of question. I have been amazed over and over at the sophisticated thinking that even preschoolers are capable of with practice and with skillful instruction and support from caring teachers who make intellectually rigorous learning enjoyable.

I suggested to this teacher that if the students had their books with them outside, it would make the task clearer and easier to grasp. He could then show them a strategy for figuring out what colors are not in the book. Learning to think at higher levels takes time and needs a good deal of support along the way. I encouraged him to persist and assured him that if he continues to ask these types of questions and continues to scaffold their thinking, the students will soon be able to answer even more challenging questions.

About a month later, I received the following email. (The teacher is not a native English speaker but is highly educated and literate in several West African languages.)

Dear Dr. Saifer,

Thank you for good idea about asking harder questions. I tried every day, but they still not get it until a few days ago. I got an idea that I should make it really easy and so when we sit down for snack I put nothing on table. I said eat the snack. Some children laughed but most were worried. So I said what's missing? Then they said snack, juice, food. So I brought the juice and food. They said but we need cups. But you didn't say cups were missing I said and now more laughed and so I got the cups. Then they asked for plates. Again I said they didn't say plates. The next day I did the same thing but this time I said tell me everything that's missing. And they did it! With only a little help. I want to keep asking more hard questions. Can you give more ideas?

How to Use This Book

This book is both theoretical and practical. Based on recent social science and neurological research findings, I posit a theory that children's thinking and adults' thinking are more alike than different. This challenges many historical beliefs about the capabilities and learning needs of our youngest students. Much of the book focuses on the implications of this theory for improving classroom practices. I provide the rationale, specific techniques, and motivation to intentionally teach young learners a range of HOT skills by incorporating them into nearly every activity and lesson. Promoting HOT skills is a way to recharge the methodology of any curriculum, regardless of its content or approach. The ideas in this book are aimed at laying the foundation for achieving the long-term goal of having all students use the full range of HOT skills in all aspects of their lives. We want this generation of children to enjoy intellectually challenging work and play now and for the rest of their lives. We want them to grow up to be a literate and wise generation who will create a society based on honesty, compassion, fairness, and equity.

The first part of the book focuses on understanding thinking in general and higher-order thinking specifically. While more theoretical than the second part, it still includes many examples of good practices in the classroom. The second part of the book focuses on strategies and techniques for helping young learners develop and use higher-order thinking.

Most of the suggested activities in this book are designed to make teaching more effective by engaging students' higher-order thinking in the process of learning content. There is at least one activity for every content area (see the chart "Activities Cross-Referenced by Content Area" in the appendix). The activities in this book use either no materials or materials that are recycled, free, or inexpensive. There are four types of activities in this book:

- enjoyable games that promote higher-order thinking called *ThinkinGames*
- curriculum ideas and teaching and learning strategies called *Cognitivities* (a combination of cognitive and activity)
- scenarios that describe teachers' lessons and interactions with students to promote their higher-order thinking called *SnapsHOTs*
- theme ideas that lend themselves to promoting higher-ordering thinking called *HOT Themes*

Nearly all young learners are capable of every type of HOT skill, but for these skills to fully develop, they need to be practiced daily and guided by caring teachers with the knowledge and skills to facilitate them. I strongly believe that the development of students' HOT skills is the X factor in our education system. It is a key strategy for closing the achievement gap and improving the academic performance of all students. Curriculum activities that require students to use HOT skills will be meaningful and challenging. Meaningful and challenging activities motivate students and engage them in learning. Motivated students engaged with a challenging curriculum is the formula for student achievement and academic success, as well as success in life. While increasing the amount of higher-order thinking would not eliminate all the challenges in our schools, it would move us significantly in the right direction and help many, many more students succeed. ⬡

Part 1
Thinking about Thinking

Imagination is more important than knowledge. For knowledge is limited, whereas imagination embraces the entire world.

—Albert Einstein, On Cosmic Religion and Other Opinions and Aphorisms

Types of Thinking Skills:
The Tools in Our Head

Because different tasks require different types of thinking, it is important to have the ability to think in many different ways. The great humanistic psychologist Abraham Maslow said, "I suppose it is tempting, if the only tool you have is a hammer, to treat everything as if it were a nail" (1966, 15). But when we have a toolbox of thinking skills, we can apply the right type of thinking skill to the particular task at hand. Also, we can add value to nearly any task—greater enjoyment, more learning, and increased likelihood of success—by applying one (or more) higher-order thinking (HOT) skill to the task. For too many of us, there are tools in the toolbox in our heads that are not used often enough (if at all) and tools that are not used effectively. This is no fault of our own. We were not called upon to use these tools as children or as students, we did not see them being used much by others, and we were rarely given instructions and opportunities to practice how to use them. Then and now, the great majority of early primary school tasks call upon students to use lower-order thinking and, to a lesser degree, middle-order thinking. So for many teachers, it is first necessary to gain a clear understanding of these mental tools and then to learn some effective strategies that will help young learners use them effectively.

A good start to the process of mastering HOT skills is to fully understand *all* thinking skills and processes as well as how they relate to and connect with each other.

A Taxonomy of Thinking Skills (TOTS)

Taxonomies are schemas that capture the essence of complex concepts by summarizing and visually organizing the main ideas. They show the relationships between the ideas by categorizing and/or sequencing them. Because taxonomies communicate the meaning of complex concepts quickly and easily, they help create a shared understanding of them. In turn, this facilitates their use by practitioners, researchers, and other stakeholders.

Figure 1 shows a taxonomy for the various forms of thinking skills presented in this book. In addition, thinking processes are included to provide the full picture necessary to turn the ideas into effective teaching and learning practices. These four common thinking processes involve the use of a variety of thinking skills in all three categories.

The order of the thinking skills in the TOTS represents a continuum from practical thinking skills to conceptual thinking skills (from the bottom of the chart to the top). Practical thinking skills are task oriented, purposeful, and utilitarian. Conceptual thinking skills are process oriented, more concerned with ideas than accomplishments, and openended. Conceptual thinkers know that a tomato is actually a fruit, but practical thinkers know not to put it in a fruit salad!

Taxonomies are developed to create common agreement about the meaning and use of terms. Terminology about thinking skills can be problematic. For example, the terms *critical thinking, reasoning,* and *analytical thinking* are sometimes used to mean higher-order thinking in general rather than specific and distinct types of higher-order thinking. Some terms used to describe thinking have different colloquial meanings than their technical meanings, such as *analyze, calculate,* and *generate.* The TOTS addresses these problems by labeling all main thinking concepts with distinct, accurate terms that are clearly defined.

How is this taxonomy different from Bloom's taxonomy? Most educators are familiar with the original Bloom's taxonomy (Bloom et al. 1956) or the revised version (Krathwohl 2002) shown in figure 2 on page 12. Bloom's taxonomy conveys the concept that there are six different levels of knowing and teachers should strive to give their students knowledge at the highest levels. Bloom and his

FIGURE 1
TAXONOMY OF THINKING SKILLS (TOTS)

Conceptual thinking

Higher-Order Thinking (HOT):
Critical and Creative Thinking Skills
Information is transformed and created

Critical Thinking Skills	**Creative Thinking Skills**
Information is transformed	*Information is created*
Parse	Imagine
Evaluate	Interpret/Synthesize
Infer	Induce/Theorize
Shift perspective	Reframe
Transfer	Generate

CONTINUUM

Middle-Order Thinking (MOT): Logical Thinking Skills
Information is utilized

Characterize

Associate/Differentiate

Categorize

Sequence/Pattern

Calculate

Connect causes and effects

Represent

Deduce

Practical thinking

Lower-Order Thinking (LOT): Functional Thinking Skills
Information is taken in

Imitate/Copy

Follow rules and directions

Memorize/Remember/Recall

Know or do by rote

Identify/Quantify

Key Thinking Processes

Choose/Make decision

Solve problems

Plan/Strategize

Analyze

FIGURE 2
BLOOM'S TAXONOMY: ORIGINAL AND REVISED

Original	Revised
Evaluation	Creating
Synthesis	Evaluating
Analysis	Analyzing
Application	Applying
Comprehension	Understanding
Knowledge	Remembering

colleagues did not refer to them as thinking skills, although they are sometimes described as such by others.

The Taxonomy of Thinking Skills (TOTS) and Bloom's taxonomy complement each other. The TOTS describes the cognitive skills and processes that underlie and produce the levels of knowledge in Bloom's taxonomy. They share the same values about learning: students should have a thorough and deep understanding of content and the ability to think critically and creatively.

The TOTS describes the wide array of thinking skills that people of all ages use in a variety of circumstances and for many different purposes. It applies to teaching and learning, but it is not tied to the field of education, as is Bloom's taxonomy.

One Snack, Many Types of Thinking

To help with understanding the Taxonomy of Thinking Skills, here is an example of how a preschool teacher might interact with four- and five-year-olds at snacktime. Consider the following questions that the teacher could ask:

1. "Are there four people at your table?"

2. "How many people are at your table?"

3. "How many napkins do you need at your table?"

4. "Are there enough plates for everyone at your table?" "How many more do you need?"

5. "What is missing from the snack table?"

6. "What snack do you eat at home that we have never had at school?"

7. "Look carefully at the bowl of crackers. Estimate how many crackers you think are there."

8. "How are crackers made and who makes them? What are the ingredients? How would you make crackers at home?"

9. "If you invented a new delicious, healthy snack, what would it be? One rule: It can't be a cracker!"

How are these questions related? What pattern do they form? The list above is a continuum that starts with a question that prompts lower-order thinking—there is only one right answer out of two possibilities (yes or no), and each subsequent question prompts a more conceptual thinking skill or a more advanced level of thinking. The second question also has one right answer, but there are more than two possible answers. The fourth question requires the logical thinking skill of calculating. The fifth question invokes the logical thinking skill of deduction, using tangible, visible items, while the question that follows entails items that are intangible. This question also requires the recall of two different items simultaneously—snacks at home and snacks at school. The final question asks the children to be creative and generate new ideas.

All HOT skills are not necessarily more difficult or better than all LOT skills. Every thinking skill can be done at a level that ranges from very basic to very advanced. (Examples of thinking at various levels of complexity are provided throughout this book.) While some tasks require LOT skills almost exclusively, such as memorizing a friend's home address (basic level) or a long formal speech (more advanced level), even these tasks can be made more interesting and easier to accomplish with the addition of HOT skills. Associating the street name and house with something already known and with an image (imagining is a creative thinking HOT skill) is an effective aid to memory. The address 1429 Pierce Drive is more easily committed to memory by associating it with "in 1492, a dyslexic Columbus *pierced* the notion that the world was flat!" Practicing a lengthy speech while imagining being in a conversation with a friend over coffee gives it a context, making it easier to memorize, as well as helping the speech sound more natural.

> Teaching and learning activities should focus on helping all students learn new, more conceptual thinking skills and move each thinking skill from its current level to more advanced levels.

Nevertheless, activities that only engage LOT skills and basic-level MOT skills predominate in most preschool and early primary classrooms and in curriculum guides. And when teachers and curriculum developers do attempt to promote HOT skills, the activities are too often confusing or difficult rather than challenging. This is easily remedied, however, once teachers have an understanding of higher-order thinking; examples of rigorous and engaging strategies and activities that promote such thinking; and enough time to practice them and gain some expertise.

While the examples of activities in this book primarily cover pre-K through third grade (ages four through eight), many apply to older or more advanced students, or can easily be modified to do so. There are also examples of how adults, particularly teachers, use and apply thinking skills. All the terms, categories, and concepts in the taxonomy related to LOT, MOT, and HOT skills, as well as to the four thinking processes, are explained in chapters 2 through 5.

Conclusion

All three of the main categories of thinking skills—lower-order, middle-order, and higher-order thinking—are important and necessary. However, our increasingly complex and rapidly changing world requires the ability to think critically and creatively at advanced levels, as well as logically and practically. Teachers, especially teachers of young learners, have an important role to play in developing their students' higher-order thinking abilities. While many teachers face obstacles to HOT teaching in the form of curriculum mandates, student testing, teacher performance expectations, district policies, and the need for training, there are still many ways that every teacher can promote their students' higher-order thinking. This chapter provides a start on developing this ability by describing, organizing, and categorizing the full range of thinking skills, as visually represented by the Taxonomy of Thinking Skills (TOTS).

The types of questions teachers ask can promote different types of thinking, as illustrated in the snacktime example in this chapter. With this understanding, teachers can become more aware of their questioning strategies so they can vary them and, ultimately, be able to ask increasingly sophisticated questions that engage students' higher-order thinking. Questioning is just one strategy for promoting HOT skills, but it is an important one because teachers ask many questions throughout the day.

Key Ideas from This Chapter

- It is important to have the ability to use a wide range of thinking skills and apply them effectively.

- Higher-order thinking is underdeveloped in most people because it has not been, and is still not, sufficiently promoted in schools, if at all.

- The ability to use higher-order thinking at advanced levels is increasingly important as our world becomes ever more complex.

- The Taxonomy of Thinking Skills (TOTS) describes three main categories of thinking skills: lower-order thinking (LOT), middle-order thinking (MOT), and higher-order thinking (HOT).

- Higher-order thinking is composed of critical and creative thinking skills. Middle-order thinking involves eight types of logical thinking skills. Lower-order thinking is made up of five practical thinking skills. The TOTS also describes four key thinking processes: Choose/Make decisions, Solve problems, Plan/Strategize, and Analyze. These processes entail the use of thinking skills in all three categories.

- Taxonomies explain complex concepts visually and succinctly.

- The TOTS and Bloom's taxonomy complement each other. The TOTS describes the thinking skills and processes that lead to the learning outcomes described in Bloom's taxonomy.

Questions for Discussion

- Describe some examples in your own schooling of tasks that you were asked to do as assignments, homework, and so on. Which categories of thinking skills did they engage?

- What were you taught about thinking skills or the role of thinking in education in your professional coursework or training?

- What are some of the specific barriers to promoting higher-order thinking that you face as a parent and/or educator? Discuss some ways these barriers can be overcome.

- Discuss ways that questions asked of students can be worded to promote critical and creative thinking.

Lower-Order Thinking (LOT) Skills:
Functional . . . If Not Always Fun

Lower-order thinking uses and relies on information as it is. It is not altered, manipulated, acted upon, or transformed. LOT skills are at the "practical" end of the practical to conceptual continuum, as shown on the Taxonomy of Thinking Skills. While it may appear that LOT skills are inferior to HOT skills, it is more accurate to understand them as functional skills, as they are useful, necessary, and, of course, practical. They are also foundational for many middle-order and higher-order skills and thinking processes. Critical reflection, for example, starts with reviewing events (remember/recall).

LOT skills are like a toolbox of basic tools: a hammer, wrenches, a drill, screwdrivers, and pliers. They are necessary and effective for accomplishing many common household tasks. HOT skills are the power tools and specialized hand tools in the toolbox that, along with the basic tools, provide the means to fix or to build just about anything—if you know how to use them!

Lower-Order Thinking (LOT) Skills
Imitate/Copy

Imitating or copying is simply reproducing something that is already fully formed, known, and evident. The goal of such activities is usually to make the most accurate reproduction possible. Requesting that students repeat what a teacher says or does elicits this type of thinking. A basic form of imitating is an activity song like "Head, Shoulders, Knees, and Toes." Learning an intricate dance is a more advanced form of imitation. An example of basic copying is when students are given a paper with a letter or shape to reproduce. Accurately reproducing the style of a particular artist is a more advanced form of copying.

Follow Rules and Directions

This is among the most common type of thinking that students do in classrooms at all grade levels, particularly in early childhood classrooms. "Hang up your coat, pick out a book, and sit quietly in the circle time area" is an example of giving students directions to follow. As children become readers, written rules and directions start replacing or supplementing verbal instructions. One intended goal of homework for early primary students is to help them learn to follow directions more independently, although too often it fails to achieve that goal (Center for Public Education 2007). An example of a more advanced level of following rules is knowing and applying traffic safety rules related to crossing streets and riding a bicycle, which is a challenge that eight-year-olds in many communities start to take on.

Following rules and directions are the thinking skills used for organizing and arranging tasks, such as filing papers alphabetically or creating a table of contents. Because the criteria and sequence for these tasks are concrete, defined, and predetermined, they only require lower-order thinking (following directions). Tasks for which the organizing criteria need to be developed or are abstract (grouping folk tales by their themes, for example) require middle- and higher-order thinking, particularly categorizing, a logical thinking skill.

Following rules and directions and organizing are important school skills, necessary for tracking when assignments are due, how the assignments are to be done, and protocols for turning in and getting feedback for assignments. Later, they are important life skills for success at work, maintaining a clean driving record, paying taxes on time, and much more.

Memorize/Remember/Recall

From the perspective of learning, memorizing is the act of intentionally knowing and retaining particular information because it is important or useful. Remembering is calling to mind the memorized information, and recalling is expressing the information verbally, in writing, or with actions. This sequence is another very common lower-order thinking task that teachers ask of their students. Spelling and vocabulary tests and learning multiplication facts involve memorizing, remembering, and recalling. In pre-K programs, memorizing, remembering, and recalling classroom rules, songs, fingerplays, and routines are common expectations of children. *Reciting* is a term for using language when recalling something that was memorized. Students are recalling and reciting when they answer such factual questions as "When is your birthday?" and "What is your address?"

When students respond to questions about what they did earlier in the day or over the weekend, or what happened on the playground to cause a conflict, they are remembering and recalling at a more advanced level. They describe or explain rather than recite, as they have to select aspects of the event that are salient to them and formulate what they will say. Although this is often done automatically, it provides the opportunity for teachers to help students remember more deliberately, to describe the event in greater detail and more comprehensively. Remembering in detail is an important first step in thinking processes such as problem solving and analyzing. Teachers can engage a student's higher-order thinking during a memory/recall activity by asking questions such as "What was the most challenging part of yesterday's game for you?" This elicits critical thinking, specifically self-evaluation or critical reflection.

Know or Do by Rote

This is a type of memorizing in which students can give correct information or perform a skill correctly, without understanding its purpose or meaning. It is common for young preschoolers to recite the alphabet without knowing the function of letters in creating words, or to count to ten without understanding that each number represents a unique quantity and that its value is relational to other numbers (called *number sense*). It can appear from the surface behavior that a child understands a concept or has a skill, when she actually is just demonstrating rote knowledge or behavior. Teachers would need to ask a particular type of question such as "Let's count these cups: one, two, three, four . . . what comes next?" "Here are three blocks. How many will you have if we add one more?" or "Now that you counted that you have ten raisins, if you give one to me, how many will you have?"

A student who understands (has number sense) will be able to answer most of these questions without recounting.

Identify/Quantify

Identifying is the thinking skill used to collect observable information, while quantifying refers to collecting numerical information. Identifying and quantifying are the thinking skills used when the information is predetermined, inherent, or obvious. Listing all the characters in a story and stating how many there are uses identification and quantification thinking. However, identifying the main character requires the logical thinking (MOT) skill of characterizing to determine and apply the criteria that makes a character a main character.

Tasks that require students to identify information are very common in schools, particularly for older students, such as reading books or articles in order to write a report about a famous person or to make a speech about how to care for a pet. Looking through a chapter in a textbook to find the answers to the questions listed at the end of the chapter is another example of an identification task. When students are asked to compare and contrast and are given the criteria (for example, compare and contrast the shapes, colors, and textures of a maple leaf and an oak leaf), it is an identification task. When the criteria need to be determined, it is a MOT task (characterizing). As with the other LOT skills, identifying can be done at advanced levels involving sophisticated instruments, such as identifying molecules with an atomic force microscope or galaxies with a giant optical space telescope.

Quantifying—counting and measuring—is a mathematical form of identifying. We are hardwired, at least to some degree, to understand and learn math. However, in infants, these concepts are very general. They can only make distinctions that are overt and cannot, for example, sense that five objects are more than four objects (Brannon and Park 2015). Quantifying can involve the use of instruments such as scales or tape measures. Even a sophisticated instrument that requires specialized knowledge and skills, such as an X-ray machine, elicits lower-order thinking if the task consists of calibrating the instrument and reading results rather than calculating, evaluating, synthesizing, or interpreting results. Identifying and quantifying are, nevertheless, important skills. They are often the necessary initial step for the four key thinking processes: problem solving, choosing/decision making, planning/strategizing, and analyzing.

Conclusion

All lower-order thinking skills involve using existing information and applying it directly. The information is not used for other purposes, connected with other information, adapted, or transformed. Nevertheless, LOT skills are very important and necessary. We use these skills every day, and being good at them is an advantage, particularly for certain tasks such as learning to drive, studying for a test, following a map, or cooking from a recipe. In some cases, LOT skills are used to accomplish some very challenging tasks that few people can do, such as learning a Beethoven sonata or memorizing all of Hamlet's lines. LOT skills are necessary but not necessarily easy! LOT skills often complement MOT and HOT skills and are often necessary initiators of thinking processes.

Helping students develop better lower-order thinking skills should be part of every teacher's job and every curriculum. However, it should be a relatively small part. In most classrooms, students spend much more time using LOT skills than HOT skills. It should be just the reverse. So I urge educators to teach "a little LOT and a lot of HOT!"

Key Ideas from This Chapter

- There are five LOT skills: imitate/copy, follow rules and directions, memorize/remember/recall, know or do by rote, and identify/quantify.

- LOT skills are important, practical, functional, and necessary.

- LOT skills are often required in the initial steps of the four key thinking processes.

- LOT skills can be difficult and challenging, such as memorizing all of Hamlet's lines.

- Most common teaching and learning strategies, particularly for young learners, only call upon the use of LOT skills.

Questions for Discussion

- What are some of the historical, social, and cultural reasons that LOT teaching and learning tasks predominate in most classrooms?

- For some of the learning outcomes or standards expected of your students, how can you determine if students understand the concepts or just know them by rote?

- What are ways that teachers can make necessary LOT tasks, such as memorizing facts or math algorithms, more meaningful and enjoyable to students?

- For students who find certain LOT skills challenging (for example, they are disorganized or have trouble remembering due dates), what can teachers do to help them compensate?

Middle-Order Thinking (MOT) Skills:
The Logical Path to Wisdom

Middle-order thinking (MOT) is logical thinking in all its variations. Logical thinking involves making linear, objective, and systematic connections between pieces of information, ideas, or numbers. Information is not just taken in but examined, put into use, separated, connected, and sometimes reorganized. In *Star Trek*, Leonard Nimoy's Mr. Spock is a half-human character who is an exemplar of logical thinking. In the 1991 film *Star Trek VI: The Undiscovered Country*, Mr. Spock says, "Logic is the beginning of wisdom, not the end." This is an excellent description of both the limitations and the promise of logical thinking. It also explains why it is middle-order thinking. Although the eight MOT skills are more than just functional like LOT skills, they are *not* transformative or generative like HOT skills. Logical thinking can serve as a bridge between LOT and HOT skills, which is fitting because logical thinking itself primarily deals with connections and relationships.

Characterize

Characterizing is the logical thinking skill used to determine the salient components or main features (characteristics and attributes) of something when they are discernable but not predetermined, inherent, or obvious. These tasks engage characterizing's lower-order cousin, identifying. Its higher-order cousins are inferring and parsing, which are the thinking skills used when the features need to be determined or developed. Characterizing is an important skill because it is the thinking needed to determine the criteria to use as the basis for applying other MOT skills (associating/differentiating, categorizing, and sequencing/patterning); the HOT skill of evaluating (a critical thinking skill); and all four thinking processes (choose/make decisions, solve problems, plan/strategize, and analyze). For these activities to be effective, good characterizing skills are necessary so that the criteria they rely on are accurate and complete.

One strategy to help young learners develop characterizing skills is through games such as Family Groups (page 62) and Don't Say the Word! (page 136). In these games, the core features are known, but not the category or concept they describe. An example of a Family Groups game involves students hearing or reading a list of words that includes *dogs, cats, parakeets, goldfish,* and *hamsters* and determining that "pet" is their common attribute or the category they all belong to. Don't Say the Word! entails describing an object to teammates without naming it so they will guess what it is, such as describing an umbrella without saying the word *umbrella*. This requires determining the key features that characterize umbrellas, which is characterization thinking.

The Art of Lotto game on page 26 offers many good opportunities to help students identify the salient features of paintings that characterize them, such as genre, subject, and the artist's unique style. The selected features can be fewer and more obvious for preschoolers and younger students and more nuanced and conceptual for second and third graders, including the type of media used; the main styles (abstract, impressionism, realism) and subjects (landscapes, seascapes, portraits, still lifes, scenes from myths); famous artists and their unique styles; and perspective, symmetry, and other basic artistic conventions.

Discussions about books usually include identifying the story's main ideas, themes, and messages, as well as literary elements such as plot points, plot devices, characters, setting, protagonist, antagonist, and so on. But it is important that students' abilities to characterize salient information is transferrable and not confined to literature. There should be ample opportunities to do this with films, video games, music, biographies, speeches, and historical and current events.

Associate/Differentiate (A/D)

Associative thinking makes logical connections between information, while differential thinking makes logical distinctions. A useful way to think about A/D thinking is that it describes a relationship. Delineating the various ways two comparable things are associated and connected, as well as the various ways they are distinct and unique, provides a comprehensive description of their relationship.

Associating and differentiating are the thinking skills behind the act of comparing. However, *comparing* is a problematic term because it has multiple meanings. In common usage, the meaning of comparing encompasses both associating and differentiating (also called contrasting), although *compare and contrast* is still a common phrase on standardized tests. Comparing often, but not always, involves an informal evaluation: comparing the latest smartphones and evaluating which is the best value. But there are many common activities that involve comparing without evaluating. Comparing the attributes of many breeds of horses is fascinating, even if it has no other purpose than to learn about horses. However, this meaning of *comparing* is more accurately described as juxtaposing and is a different cognitive process from evaluating. It is essentially identifying information and arranging it, which are two LOT skills, whereas comparing that evaluates is a critical thinking HOT skill.

There is yet another activity that can be described as comparing, which is making nonevaluative comparisons when the criteria are unknown, subjective, or conceptual, for example, comparing the skills and dispositions that kindergarten teachers need to be effective with those needed by second grade teachers. Or comparing four different versions of the Cinderella story for what they communicate about the culture and values of the countries from which they originate. These activities not only use A/D thinking but also the critical thinking HOT skills of inferring and parsing.

For the reasons described above, *associating* and *differentiating* are used instead of *comparing* throughout the book. This provides a more specific and clearer description of this common and important logical thinking skill.

On the following page is an activity to help students develop A/D skills by modifying a memory lotto game. Lotto games typically involve associating and differentiating at a basic level. The two cards that are turned upright are evaluated to determine if they are the same or different. In many commercially made lotto games, the task is very easy because every pair of cards has a completely different picture and each pair of cards has exactly the same picture. The focus of the game is on memorization and recall, not on the relationship between the cards that make up a pair or on the relationships among all the pairs in the set. A lotto game can be made very difficult by using a large number of pairs of cards, but it is still a LOT activity. However, when A/D thinking tasks are added to the memorization task, as in the *ThinkinGame* below, lotto games become MOT activities. In addition, activities that require students to use two or more types of thinking simultaneously help them develop the capacity to do intellectually challenging work.

THINKINGAME: THE ART OF LOTTO

This *ThinkinGame* is played like standard lotto, but the matching pairs of cards are similar, not the same. The cards are reproductions of paintings, photos of famous architectural structures (such as the Eiffel Tower and the Pyramids of Giza), and photos of sculptures. For preschoolers, the paintings should be representational with subjects of interest to them, such as children, animals, boats, and trains. In the basic version of the game, a matched pair consists of paintings of the same genre or style. The pairs range from very similar and easy to match (such as paintings by the same artist) to significantly different but clearly of the same genre. There are tens of thousands of high-quality images of paintings and photographs available through the Creative Commons website (https://creativecommons.org) that can be used for this game.

Each set of art lotto cards needs to contain a large number of pairs of diverse art and several duplicates of the same card. Sets also need multiple pairs of paintings of the same genre to make the game more challenging. A large set of cards can be separated into subsets for different levels of challenge and versions of the game.

One variation of the game is to include duplicates of the same card as well as cards that are similar. A matched pair consists of similar cards, not the same cards. Adding such counterintuitive elements to games helps students develop impulse control and learn to avoid thinking errors. Once students are adept at the basic version, the criterion for what constitutes a match is changed. This requires selecting cards to create a set that will work with the new criterion. For example, a match can consist of paintings that have the same number of people in them (including zero). Now, matched pairs will be of different genres of art. Students have to reframe (a creative thinking skill) the focus of their observations while looking at the same images. Another criterion that can be used to match paintings is the main subject of the painting: people, animals, flowers, food, trains, boats, and so on. Yet another criterion is the media used: oils, watercolors, charcoal, pastels, ink, pencil.

When teachers make their own lotto cards from postcards, pictures from magazines or brochures, fair-use photos from the internet, or their own drawings and photos, they can create cards with meaningful content for their students at the right level of challenge. The cards can also reflect a theme or content area of knowledge, such as types of birds or basic geography.

FIGURE 3
LOTTO ART CARDS SAMPLE

Seascape with Lighthouse, James Bulwer, British

Breezing Up (A Fair Wind), Winslow Homer, 1873–1876, American

Self-Portrait with White Collar, Edgar Degas, 1857, French

Self-Portrait, Vincent van Gogh, 1889, Dutch

Still Life of Oranges and Lemons with Blue Gloves, Vincent van Gogh, 1889, Dutch

Still Life, Henri Fantin-Latour, 1866, French

Sunrise in the Catskills, Thomas Cole, 1826, American

Brittany Landscape, Paul Gauguin, 1888, French

Categorize

Categorizing entails grouping three or more items by one or more shared attribute. Attributes used to categorize can be physical (shape, size, color) or abstract (usefulness, importance, worth). Overt attributes employ basic-level categorizing, while abstract attributes engage more advanced categorization thinking skills.

Categorizing activities should be purposeful. When a preschool student separates and groups all the colored pencils according to color, he is making it easier for everyone to find and access their desired color. If there are ten different colors, then the task consists of categorizing one element (a pencil) by one physical attribute (color) with ten factors (the ten colors). A first-grade student categorizes by two attributes when she chooses to group pictures of dinosaurs (the element) by their main physical attribute (armored, horned, or long-necked) and then by the slightly more abstract attribute of what they ate (plant eater, meat eater, or omnivore). Here, there is one element with two attributes, and each attribute has three factors. The complexity of a categorizing task is determined by the complexity of the element, the number of attributes, the number of factors, and the level of abstraction. A dinosaur is a more abstract element than a pen. Unlike a pen, an actual dinosaur cannot be seen and held and there are many more types of dinosaurs than types of pens. And nonvisible or nonphysical attributes and factors (what a dinosaur ate) are more abstract than visible or physical ones (a dinosaur's horn or the color of a pen).

Following are additional examples of categorizing at three different levels, from more basic to more advanced. There are, of course, many levels in between, as well as some below and above, that have not been included. Also, there are numerous other ways to categorize the items at each level. Nonetheless, these examples illustrate levels of complexity as they relate to a thinking skill, in this case, categorizing.

Marbles (Children about Four Years Old)

This example illustrates categorizing one physical element by two physical attributes. One attribute has two factors and the other has four.

A box contains twenty-six marbles (the element). The marbles are identical except for their colors and sizes (the attributes). The task for two preschoolers is to categorize them by size and color in preparation for a game. From previous experience playing marbles, they know they each need six small marbles (targets) and one large marble (a shooter) of the same color to start the game. Four of the marbles in the box are large and twenty-two are small. Small and large are the two factors of the size attribute. There are four different colors among the marbles:

orange, red, green, and blue (the four factors of the color attribute). Each of the four large marbles is a different color. Six of the twenty-two small marbles are orange, four are red, five are green, and seven are blue. Although one student wants to use green marbles, they figure out together that the only choices are orange and blue.

Beads (Children about Five Years Old)

In this example, there is a physical element with three physical attributes that have two to four factors.

A box contains about one hundred beads (the element) of various sizes, colors, and composition. There are three factors for the size attribute: small, medium, and large. There are four factors for the color attribute: red, blue, green, and multicolored. And two factors make up the composition attribute: glass and ceramic. The task is to sort the beads by their size and color (two of the attributes) in preparation for making a necklace for name badges to use in an upcoming field trip. The result is twelve sets of beads. To keep them well organized, students put each set in a small jar and then sequence the jars in this order: small red beads, medium red beads, large red beads, small blue beads, medium blue beads, large blue beads, small green beads, medium green beads, large green beads, small multicolored beads, medium multicolored beads, and finally, large multicolored beads. Because there is a random mix of beads, the number of beads in each set varies.

Trees (Children about Eight Years Old)

The following *SnapsHOT* involves categorizing a physical element with three abstract attributes that each have multiple factors. Some of the factors are physical and some are abstract.

SNAPSHOT: FREE THE TREES!

To express their unhappiness about a plan to cut down trees around the school to make room for more parking spaces, second-grade students decide they need to learn as much as they can about the trees on the demolition list. Facilitated by the teacher, they make a large chart (see figure 4) listing each of the seven trees (the element) with three categories of information about them (the attributes) as follows:

FIGURE 4
TREE CHART

	European Linden	**American Beech**	**Northern Red Oak**
Seven Trees			
Leaves, Nuts, Flowers, Sap	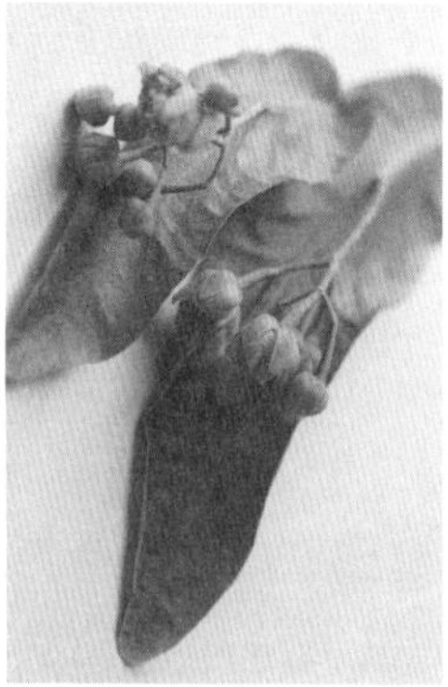		
Description	VERY BIG, leaves turn yellow & fall off, small yellow blossoms in spring	Grows slowly, branches spread wide, leaves turn gold & orange, makes nuts	VERY BIG, leaves turn red & fall off, grows fast, makes acorns in fall & catkins in spring
Material Value	Dried blossoms make tea good for tummy aches, also smell good for air fresheners	Makes beechnuts, which you can eat	Use acorns for math and science activities
Intangible Value	Shade, beauty, smells good, birds singing, aids air quality	Shade, pretty in the fall, birds, air quality, great for climbing (if allowed)	Shade, pretty in the fall, home to lots of squirrels & birds, air quality

Blue Spruce (x2)	Sugar Maple	Black Walnut
Evergreen, silvery blue color, tall, big pine cones, sharp prickly needles	Big tree, bright red leaves in fall, "helicopter" pods with two seeds, sap makes syrup	Tall tree, spicy smell, leaves turn yellow, dark bark, walnut shells leave stains, toxic to other trees
Decorate for winter fest and not buy trees, cones for math & science, decorations, fire starters	Maple syrup	Walnuts, brown dye
Pretty all year, winter fest trees, shelter for birds and squirrels, blocks wind	Shade, beauty (especially in fall), squirrels & birds, air quality	Shade, beauty, squirrels and birds, air quality

1. Description: the type of tree, its origins, history, and main characteristics (four or more factors)

2. Material value: the usefulness of the tree when it's alive and growing, such as the fruits and nuts it bears; its role in counteracting air pollution; and the medicinal proprieties of its leaves, bark, and/or flowers (three or more factors)

3. Intangible value: the tree's contribution to the well-being and happiness of the students, staff, and people in the neighborhood, such as its shade; color and beauty; good smells; the habitat it provides for birds and squirrels; and its role in the local ecosystem (five or more factors)

To get this information about the trees, the teacher asks questions, facilitates discussions, provides relevant books, websites, and films, and recruits colleagues and friends who have more expertise in ecology and dendrology (the study of woody plants and trees) to talk with the students. Then the class makes a display with photographs and a chart that summarizes the information they collected about the trees. They are looking forward to presenting the information at an upcoming joint meeting of the school board and the town council.

Sequence/Pattern

Sequencing is a particularly important thinking skill for young learners. They need to be able to track and recall a story or describe a series of events in the correct order. For something to be a sequence, it has to have at least three components, such as a beginning, middle, and end. Sequencing is also an important aspect of math for tracking ordinal numbers, keeping numbers in their appropriate place value columns, and similar math skills.

Sequencing commands in a computer program requires an advanced level of this skill. Yet educators and researchers at MIT created an app that enables children as young as five to program a computer. Using a touch-screen tablet, students sequence icons, each of which represents a basic computer command, to create their own unique interactive stories and simple computer games (see "Technology," pages 126–128, for more information on ScratchJr).

Prioritizing is an important type of sequencing skill. It is a main thinking skill for planning/strategizing, which is a key thinking process. Prioritizing is sequencing based on the broad criterion of importance, expedience, or a similar factor. However, what is deemed important or who expediency benefits is subjective and personal.

Forming patterns is a special type of sequencing, although deciphering patterns is done with another type of logical thinking, characterizing. Patterning can be as basic as creating a necklace with the repeated pattern of two black beads followed by two red beads or as advanced as weaving a tapestry. When the creative thinking skills of imagining and generating ideas are applied to patterning, it becomes designing. As there are patterns in written and spoken language, mathematics, daily routines, human behaviors, life cycles, and so much more, having good thinking skills for patterning is a valuable cognitive asset.

Calculate

Calculating involves arithmetic computations: adding, subtracting, multiplying, and dividing. Adding single digit numbers is the simplest form of calculation. The ability to calculate accurately, fluently, and consistently, even at this basic level, requires students to have numerical understanding, or number sense. And having number sense is a prerequisite for understanding more-advanced math. Number sense comes with the understanding that a number is more than a representation of an amount. There are logical relationships among numbers; a number has differential value relative to the numbers below it and above it. This should be the focus of many math activities for young learners because it moves such activities from engaging LOT skills (rote counting, memorizing algorithms) to engaging logical thinking MOT skills.

Activities that involve playing with numbers when done often and regularly and with increasing challenge will develop math ability at a deeper level and more effectively and enjoyably than practicing pencil and paper math problems. For example, the math *ThinkinGame* Twins, on page 134, and all its variations give students direct experience with the concept that the same number can be a high number or low number and a winning number or losing number.

Calculating is the purest form of logical thinking, as there is always one right answer and the logic of an equation is not obfuscated by words, ideas, or other messy things with multiple or fuzzy meanings. However, poorly conceived word problems and test directions can do an excellent job of obfuscating a simple calculation task. More-advanced math, such as algebra and statistics, requires the HOT skills of inferring, inducing/theorizing, and interpreting/synthesizing, in addition to calculating thinking at advanced levels.

Connect Causes and Effects

Doctors often use the logic of cause and effect thinking to inform, motivate, and occasionally scare their patients: "If you take this pill once a day for ten days, your infection will go away and you will feel better." "If you don't lose weight, you may develop diabetes." "Put ice on your sprain to reduce the swelling and pain." "Using sunscreen reduces your risk of getting skin cancer."

It is important for young students to understand the relationships between a variety of causes and effects, particularly those that are not immediate, in order to develop social skills, understand science concepts, delay gratification, and much more. Delaying gratification and achieving long-term goals require an understanding that there is often a time gap between a cause and an effect. Putting effort into learning to read in first grade will lead to being able to keep up with schoolwork in later grades. It will give students more autonomy because they will be able to read independently for pleasure and information. And reading with fluency means getting assignments done quickly, which will give them more leisure time.

The ability to give clear explanations and justifications requires a good understanding of cause and effect relationships. When young students respond to questions such as "What might have happened to cause . . ." and "What could happen if . . .," they practice connecting causes and effects.

Cause and effect relationships are at the heart of many science concepts, such as gravity, evolution, and how simple machines work, viruses spread, and the Grand Canyon was formed. Understanding cause and effect relationships is necessary to comprehend and track the sequence of events and plotlines in books and films. When students are guided to focus on cause and effect relationships during a wide variety of activities, they gain a conceptual understanding and can begin to apply the concept in different contexts. Such activities include building a tower with blocks until it falls over and then using the same number of blocks to build it again in a different way so it won't fall over; creating a Rube Goldberg contraption; learning about major historical events and their causes and effects; using software such as Crayon Physics (http://crayonphysics.com); and conducting investigations to explore how altering a variable or an input changes an effect. There is an example of a preschooler exploring causes and effects with water, funnels, and containers in the *SnapsHOT* Go with the Flow, on page 159.

Cause and effect relationships also explain much of the dynamics of social interactions. When students understand the many ways their behavior affects others and how the behaviors of others affect them, they become more self-aware and better able to mediate their emotions. Even preschoolers can begin to gain these insights, particularly with the help of delightful and perceptive children's literature, as described below.

SNAPSHOT: LILLY

Each year in May, Ms. Angel, a preschool teacher, implements the theme "What Happens in Kindergarten at the Big School?" Among the activities is reading high-quality children's literature with stories that take place in kindergarten and first-grade classrooms. *Lilly's Purple Plastic Purse* (Henkes 2006a) is always a favorite.

Lilly, the irrepressible mouse heroine of the story, adores her teacher, Mr. Slinger, so much that she wants to be a teacher when she grows up. However, when she shows off her musical purple plastic purse at inappropriate times, Mr. Slinger confiscates it for the day. Lilly's humiliation causes her to be angry, which she vents by drawing a mean picture of Mr. Slinger, while deciding that she no longer wants to be a teacher. But a kind note and yummy snack from Mr. Slinger found in her returned purse causes her to regret the drawing and feel a deep sense of remorse. Fortunately, Lilly's sincere apology along with a new *nice* drawing of Mr. Slinger and gift of a yummy snack of her own have their intended effect. Mutual admiration is restored, and, once again, Lilly wants to be a teacher.

One of the follow-up activities to the story is identifying all the cause and effect relationships. Ms. Angel uses a variety of photos and graphics that illustrate different types of cause and effect relationships to start a discussion. She has photo sets with a single cause and a single effect such as a snowman melting in the sun. She has photo sets with a series of causes and effects: an empty dog food bowl, a sad dog, a full dog food bowl, a happy dog; photo sets with one cause and multiple effects: a photo of snow falling and photos of a person shoveling snow, children making a snow sculpture, and children sledding; and sets showing multiple causes and a single effect: a photo of a child with a music trophy in one hand and a violin in the other and photos of him practicing at home, getting a lesson from his teacher, attending a concert played by a professional violinist, listening to music with headphones, playing with a friend who is playing a cello, and performing in the competition.

Ms. Angel reviews the story with the children starting from the end. She uses the photo of the sun to represent the concept of cause and the melting snowman to represent the concept of effect. Ms. Angel asks questions such as "What did Lilly do that caused Mr. Slinger and Lilly to be happy and be friends again?"

Second and third graders are ready to understand that one effect can have several causes and that a number of effects can result from a single cause, at a more abstract and advanced level, as in the example below:

SNAPSHOT: DROUGHT

In a third-grade classroom, the severe drought and its repercussions is a hot topic among the students. They talk about not being able to swim because of the lack of water in the lakes and rivers, about neighbors who are not following the rules for saving water, and about the water fountains being shut off. The teacher elicits and supports their cause and effect thinking to deepen their understanding of the science and ecology of the drought.

She discovers that the students believe there is only one cause for not having enough water: a lack of rain. She tells them, "That is one cause, but there are others." On the whiteboard, she draws a cloud with rain coming down with a red line through it and writes, "1. Lack of rain." Underneath she draws a picture of a faucet with drops of water coming down and a house with grass around it. "What might be another cause?" she asks. After a brief discussion, she writes, "2. Using and wasting too much water," and says, "For the last ten years, a few years before you were born, until now, if everyone used just a little less water and if there were no lawns, which need a lot of water, we would probably not have a water shortage now." While drawing a picture of a barn, she tells the students, "Here's a hint for another cause. This one is hard." After no one can come up with an answer, she says, "Another cause is that we have many, many farms in our area, and it takes a great amount of water to grow nuts, fruits, and vegetables." On the whiteboard, she writes, "3. Farms." "So, there are at least three causes for our water shortage: the lack of rain, using too much water at home and for lawns, and the large amount of water that farms need to use. A big, complicated problem, like not having enough water, usually has more than one cause. Also, the lack of rain has had many more effects than adding to a water shortage. It has caused many other problems, such as forest fires." She then has the students work together in small groups to determine why a lack of rain causes more forest fires and to identify as many other effects as they can.

Causes and effects are not always evident, immediate, or straightforward. One reason that punishments are ineffective is that adults assume that children can mentally connect the effect, which is the punishment, to the cause, which is the problematic behavior (although the child might not think it's problematic). Adults further assume that children will recall that particular cause and effect relationship and heed it at some future time when tempted to repeat the behavior.

Making meaning is a core mental activity for young learners, as they are actively trying to understand the world. An effective way to glean meaning about how the world works is to explore cause and effect relationships, creating them if necessary. Babies do this when they intentionally drop things from their high chairs, and children, from preschoolers through third graders, do this when they ask questions that begin with "What would happen if . . . ?" and "Would you still love me if I . . .?" In many cases, they are trying to determine if their own cause and effect thinking is faulty. Even adults sometimes believe there is a cause and effect relationship when there isn't one or fail to see a cause and effect relationship when there is one.

Represent

Pretending is perhaps the earliest representational thinking that human beings engage in. When a child pretends to be a dog, he is using his body, actions, and voice to represent a familiar animal. When a child pretends to drink water from a toy cup, he is representing the real activity with a simulated activity. The first recognizable drawings that children create—typically a stick-figure person, the sun, a house, a tree, or a flower—means that they can represent familiar three-dimensional objects in two dimensions. The level of representational thinking increases as children learn that a bunch of shapes strung together represents their names and, therefore, themselves and eventually learn that those shapes are symbols that represent the sounds in their names. At about the same time, young students learn that another set of symbols represent numbers. It is a logical thinking skill because there is a direct and linear relationship between the symbol and what it represents. Of course, many symbols represent more than one thing. The letter symbol *A* represents many sounds, a word that means "one," and a good grade on a test. Decoding symbols and coding with symbols are tasks that involve representational thinking, along with other thinking skills. With the addition of imagining and other HOT skills, representing can take many compelling forms: imaginary play, allegorical tales like Aesop's "The Tortoise and the Hare," and elements of poetry, film, and visual art. In some cases, an entire work is representational, such as the novels *Animal Farm* by George Orwell and *Lord of the Flies* by William Golding.

Graphic designers use colors, shapes, patterns, symbols, and other visual elements to represent a particular idea, feeling, or quality. The best designers use representational thinking at an advanced level: the logo or symbol of an automobile company has been very carefully designed to represent how they want consumers to perceive their cars and distinguish them from other car brands. In general, logos with a few shiny diagonal lines are used to represent speed and modernity. Logos with complex designs and multiple patterns usually represent luxury and history. Animals in logos are used to represent power. The logo of a British manufacturer of very expensive cars is a stylized, shiny chrome large jungle cat (which is also the name of the company), leaping up diagonally in midair as if ready to pounce. This image manages to represent speed, power, modernity, and luxury. Representational thinking at the highest levels can be very impactful.

Although promoting representational thinking is a major part of most curricula from preschool through second grade, often it is only applied to formal literacy and numeracy activities. These activities entail predetermined representations: every number is a symbol that represents a quantity, and every letter is a symbol that represents a sound (phoneme) or set of sounds.

Representational thinking, being a functional and practical thinking skill, as are all logical thinking skills, tends to be content specific and not readily transferrable across activities and content areas (transferring is a critical thinking skill). An effective and enjoyable strategy to help young learners simultaneously develop transferring and representational thinking skills is through games and activities that use nonstandard symbols. Using a variety of nonstandard symbols in many different activities promotes transferring skills because it conveys the *concept* of symbols rather than the meaning of particular symbols, such as letters, numbers, and familiar icons. These symbols should represent many different types of objects, concepts, and actions, including those that are not typically represented by symbols. The app ScratchJr does this elegantly. It gives children ages five to seven coding tools in the form of symbols so they can independently write computer programs to create unique interactive stories or simple games (see "Technology," pages 126–128, for more information on ScratchJr).

Scaffolded writing (Bodrova and Leong 2007; Scott-Weich and Yaden 2017) is a very effective literacy development strategy for preschoolers and kindergartners in which students draw horizontal lines to represent words. This gives preliterate children the tools to "write" messages in sentences that carry meaning and are purposeful. They draw lines as they say the words, using basic writing conventions such as left-to-right sequencing, spacing, and starting the next line by moving the pencil down and to the left margin. The teacher then writes the words under the lines while students repeat the sentence. As students learn letter sounds, they write the letters on the lines, starting with initial sounds and letters. Starting sentences with "I," as in "I want a dog," helps children transition from representational writing to actual writing, since *I* is a phoneme, a letter, and a word and is easy to write. Bodrova and Leong developed a system that uses the power of representational thinking to enable preliterate children to graphically record whole thoughts. Just as icons and symbols eliminate communication barriers caused by language differences and sign language eliminates communication barriers caused by auditory limitations, scaffolded writing eliminates communication barriers caused by developmental limitations.

The *ThinkinGame* below uses symbols chosen by the students that represent musical directions.

THINKINGAME: CONDUCTOR

Students make a set of cards with one symbol on each card. The "conductor" shows the cards to the rest of the students, who are singing a familiar song. The symbols are abstract and unrelated to the directions they represent, although some symbols can give a clue about the instructions they represent when first introducing the game. A red triangle might mean to sing a little faster, and a green circle might mean to sing a little slower. Two red triangles would indicate to sing much faster, and two green circles would indicate to sing much slower. Other symbols can indicate louder, softer, stop, start, higher, and lower. One student at a time takes a turn being the conductor, who starts by giving the "orchestra" a music lesson by reviewing the symbols and the directions they represent. The orchestra then sings, and the conductor holds up symbols in the order and for the length of time that he desires. For preschoolers and kindergartners, the symbols/directions should be simple and introduced gradually. When students become proficient, new challenges can be added, such as holding up two or more symbols at the same time (if they do not conflict) and adding symbols that represent more complex musical directions like *crescendo* (gradually getting louder), *diminuendo* (gradually getting softer), and *staccato* (choppy). Other variations are limited only by the teacher's and students' imaginations.

Deduce

Finding an answer or solution by deduction entails eliminating (deducting) all the possible answers that cannot be, or are very unlikely to be, true. People use this important thinking skill more than they realize—almost intuitively. However, using it effectively can require practice and instruction, particularly for young learners. A common use of this MOT skill is when trying to find a lost object, such as a set of car keys. We look in each place where we might have left them (in the ignition, on the kitchen counter, on top of the dresser, or in a jacket pocket, a different purse, or the pocket of the other jeans). If they are not there, we eliminate those places from our list and deduce that we must have dropped them walking between the car and building. Now, with our attention focused at ground level, we retrace our steps and find the keys where we dropped them when getting out of the car.

In his Sherlock Holmes stories, Sir Arthur Conan Doyle raised deductive thinking to a very high intellectual level. Although fictional, all of Sherlock Holmes's brilliant deductions are plausible, which is what makes the stories so compelling and enduring. The message to take away from the character of Mr. Holmes is "elementary": deductive thinking is a very powerful problem-solving tool. Rather than taking Holmes's deductions literally, they should be viewed as inspiration to use deductive thinking at the most advanced level possible.

Below is a *ThinkinGame* to promote deductive thinking, as well as categorizing, using aesthetically pleasing, natural loose parts (see "Loose Parts," pages 125–126, for more information.).

THINKINGAME: GAME OF STONES

With a small group of about four to six students, the activity starts by students carefully observing and describing the attributes of each stone among a group of small stones and organizing them by their attributes (see the first photo below). The stones are carefully chosen to be distinct from each other on at least one attribute, such as size, color, or shape. Then the stones are randomly arranged (as in the second photo) in the middle of the group of students. One student is the Stone Master, who selects one of the stones to hide in a small box or cup while the other students are not looking. Because it is difficult for many young learners to avoid looking by just closing their eyes—the temptation is too great—it may be necessary to have them turn their bodies to face away from the

FIGURE 5
GAME OF STONES

FIGURE 5
GAME OF STONES

stones or put their heads down on their folded arms. Then the students look at the stones that remain and try to figure out which stone is missing.

When a student thinks she knows the answer and can describe the stone's attributes in enough detail to distinguish it from the others, she puts her hands on her head. The first student to do so answers first. If the student is wrong or cannot describe enough of the stone's attributes to distinguish it, the second student has a turn. The Stone Master is in charge of making the call, with assistance from the teacher if needed. The student who is correct gets to be the next Stone Master.

The first few times this game is played, there should only be a few stones so students can easily learn the game and be successful at the start. For younger students, the stones can be left in an organized arrangement, as in the first photo. The number of stones, attributes, and attribute factors should vary depending on the age level and skill level of the students. For example, the photo above shows twelve stones with three attributes (shape, size, and color) and nine attribute factors. The nine factors consist of two shapes: oval and round; two sizes: small and large; and five colors: white, light gray, dark gray, black, and white with black lines (or bicolored). For all grade levels, it is important to continually increase the challenge. More challenging variations include rearranging the stones after hiding a stone, hiding more than one stone, and adding stones to increase the number of attributes (e.g., thickness and texture) and factors (e.g., thick and thin, smooth and rough, medium-sized, rectangular, and brown stones).

To get the correct answer, students need to use deductive thinking and the LOT skills of memorizing and recalling. They look at the attributes of the stones they can see and eliminate possibilities. Teachers can use or adapt the deductive thought process described below, which refers to the stones in the third photo, as a teaching tool to make deductive thinking explicit and demonstrate how it can be used to solve problems.

"There are eight oval stones now, and there were eight before, so the hidden stone has to be round. Of the four round stones that were there, two were big and two were small. Since there are two big ones here now, the hidden stone must be small and round. The one round, small stone here is light gray so the hidden stone is either white or dark gray. I'm pretty sure it was a dark color, so I'll eliminate white. I think the hidden stone is small, round, and dark gray."

Conclusion

Since there are eight distinct middle-order thinking skills, it is evident that a good deal of thinking involves logical thinking—or at least it should. Most people know when and why to think logically, know the importance and value of logical thinking, and are familiar with these eight skills, even if they're not familiar with the terminology. Nevertheless, most people have difficulty using them effectively and avoiding biases, distractions, mental laziness, and other influences that prevent or corrupt their use. Perhaps effectively using logical thinking would come easier for more people if as students they had had explicit instruction and more opportunities to practice it in a variety of situations and contexts, for many different purposes, and in all content areas.

Each logical thinking skill is the basis for the critical and creative thinking skills used in the four thinking processes (choose/make decisions, solve problems, plan/strategize, and analyze). If the basis is weak, or if the information obtained with logical thinking is faulty, applying even the most advanced critical and creative thinking skills cannot compensate and produce valid and reliable results. However, when the flexibility and openness of critical and creative thinking is fused with the strength of solid logical thinking, the pathway to wisdom is clear.

Key Ideas from This Chapter

Middle-order thinking (MOT) skills are logical thinking skills in all their forms. There are eight logical thinking skills:

- Characterize: This is the thinking used to determine the salient characteristics, or main features, of something when they are discernable but not predetermined or obvious, such as the plot, theme, protagonist, and antagonist in a story.

- Associate/Differentiate (A/D): Because the term *comparing* has multiple meanings, it is replaced by the more specific terms *associating* (making logical connections between two comparable things) and *differentiating* (making logical distinctions between two comparable things). *A/D thinking* refers to the general thinking skill used to describe the relationship between two comparable things, their similarities and differences.

- Categorize: Categorization thinking is used to group things or concepts by one or more common attribute. The attributes or purpose for categorizing is determined by the student rather than being predetermined. Categorizing can be a complex activity when there are many attributes that are abstract.

- Sequence/Pattern: Sequencing or patterning entails following a set of instructions (which may be implied rather than explicit) or a logical order, such as shortest to tallest, alphabetical order, highest value to lowest value, or most important to least (prioritizing). Patterning can be as simple and regular as a pop song's verse/chorus/verse/chorus or as complex as the recurring themes and variations in a Brahms symphony.

- Calculate: This is thinking used to perform the mathematical operations of adding, subtracting, multiplying, and dividing.

- Connect causes and effects: Cause and effect thinking involves understanding the relationship between an event and its impact(s). Young learners are developing the ability to recognize that some causes have delayed effects, some effects have multiple causes, and some causes produce multiple effects.

- Represent: Representative thinking is the ability to make a connection between something actual and a symbol that conveys its meaning. Letters represent sounds or grades, icons at airports represent information, emoticons represent feelings, and numbers represent quantities.

- Deduce: Deductive thinking is used to determine the "correct" solution or answer by eliminating other possibilities.

Logical thinking activities often form the basis for higher-order thinking activities. The criteria for making evaluations or conducting an analysis (HOT skills) are developed with logical thinking skills, and good logical thinking skills are necessary to ensure that the criteria are accurate and complete.

Questions for Discussion

- Discuss the many barriers and challenges to clear, logical thinking. How can teachers minimize these barriers for their students?

- What are the positive and negative impacts of computers and technology on human ability to think logically? Is the net effect positive or negative and why? What are some ways that technology can be used with young learners to help them develop a wide range of logical thinking skills?

- What are some of the common errors adults make in regard to connecting causes and effects? (Errors are particularly common when it comes to explaining certain scientific and natural phenomena.) What are possible reasons why so many adults make these errors? How can teachers help students avoid making such cause and effect errors?

- Students will spend many hours over many years quantifying (a LOT skill) and calculating (a MOT skill) as part of their math lessons. How can HOT skills be introduced to make the lessons more engaging and challenging, without making the problems too difficult for young learners?

Higher-Order Thinking (HOT) Skills:
Insight and Innovation

While the process of memorizing a Beethoven sonata entails a series of advanced LOT skills, only a pianist with excellent creative thinking skills (interpreting/synthesizing, especially) can play it with the sensitivity and passion that will delight and move an audience. And only an actor with excellent creative thinking skills can bring the character of Hamlet to life. Higher-order thinking is necessary to turn notes into music and words into characters. The musicians and actors with the most-advanced creative HOT skills we call artists.

The two main types of HOT skills—critical thinking and creative thinking—serve different purposes and are equally important. Critical thinking enables people to see beyond what is apparent to what is actual, what is trivial to what is vital, and to not just know but to really understand. Critical thinking skills are used, or should be used, in all four key thinking processes: choosing/decision making, problem solving, planning/strategizing, and analyzing. When creative thinking is used in the four thinking processes, the results are almost always more effective and impactful. Creative thinking is also used in common tasks such as arranging and decorating a classroom, creating engaging lesson plans, making up stories, adapting songs, resolving conflicts between students and ethical dilemmas with parents, and coming up with new ideas for activities. The ability to think creatively at advanced levels is a great benefit when undertaking these tasks.

Critical Thinking Skills: More Than Meets the Eye

The five critical thinking skills—parsing, evaluating, inferring, shifting perspective, and transferring—involve more subjective and thorough manipulation of information than logical thinking. Logical thinking is a practical thinking skill, whereas critical thinking relies more on conceptual thinking. Information is not taken at face value but instead is used, manipulated, transformed, examined, evaluated, analyzed, critiqued, and so on. There are many important purposes and goals for critical thinking, but four are crucial:

- to think clearly and accurately
- to learn for understanding
- to see beyond surface appearances
- to determine the veracity of information

Critical thinking helps to moderate one's own thinking errors and to avoid being deceived by the faulty thinking used by advertisers, politicians, salespeople, purveyors of fake news, and others. An ideal approach to critical thinking is to be skeptical but not cynical and open-minded but not gullible.

Parse

In general terms, to parse means to analyze critically, to examine something closely. But it is most often used to mean a particular type of critical analysis, the purpose of which is to uncover the deeper meaning and implications and/or to determine the veracity of something, such as a speech, behavior, or text. In addition, *parsing* can be used to mean filtering information, questioning assumptions, and seeing beyond surface appearances that may be misleading or false. However, parsing is not usually considered to mean a way of thinking; it is a verb that has no adjective form. But it does describe the act of applying this important set of related critical thinking skills, and it appears to be the only word in English that does. Logically, if analyzing is considered both an activity and a way of thinking, then a type of analyzing—which parsing clearly is—can also be considered both an activity and a way of thinking.

Researchers and computer programmers use software to parse data (take apart and rearrange large sets of information) to find structures and relationships that may reveal meanings that could not be seen when the thousands of pieces of data were in random order or organized differently. Usually the data is in numerical form, such as with test scores. This process also reveals outliers, or pieces of information that do not fit anywhere. In most cases, these outliers are mistakes. They are often keyboarding errors made when the information was entered into the computer program, such as mistakenly entering a score of two hundred although the highest possible score is one hundred. Investigative reporters and political analysts also parse information, which is often text based. The process and goals are very similar; however, thinking errors are revealed rather than numerical errors.

Parsing also describes thinking that questions assumptions and filters biases informally and quickly. Any piece of information, whether something seen, heard, or read, can be parsed: "That sure does look like a UFO! Let's parse it. Maybe it's a satellite or something like it. We can check the NASA and NOAA websites." Although not every piece of information needs to be or should be parsed, clearly parsing is an underused and underdeveloped thinking skill. Parsing is facilitated by careful observations, knowing various types of thinking errors, and by asking incisive questions. Teachers can promote the development of students' parsing skills within projects, lessons, games, and when teachable moments present themselves. When reviewing a complex story with third graders, a teacher might say, "With your partner, parse the girl's behavior and actions in the story. If you think she is pretending not to care, why would she do that? If you think she really doesn't care, what is the author's message?"

Helping students ask incisive questions (a.k.a. HOT questions) also facilitates the development of parsing. Teachers can provide students with models and examples by asking many different types of incisive questions throughout the day (see "HOT Questions: 'Roses and Thorns,'" pages 158–162, for more information). Teachers should also be responsive to students' questions and help them pose more complex, focused, and clearly stated questions. Teachers can prompt students to turn statements that infer questions into actual questions. For example, if a preschool student says, "I can't make a *Y*," the teacher can ask, "What would you like do about it?" or "Would you like to ask me a question?" If necessary, the teacher can suggest responses such as "How can I make a *Y*?" or "Can you please help me make a *Y*?"

In the following *SnapsHOT,* the teacher uses the opportunity provided by an upcoming visit to the school by a children's book author to develop his students' ability to generate incisive questions that will lead to a deep and comprehensive understanding about writing books, the work authors do, and about the books themselves.

SNAPSHOT: QUESTIONS FOR AN AUTHOR

In the weeks prior to a visit by a well-known author of children's books, Mr. Reese's first graders read several of her books and learn about her professional and personal life. They watch a short video of her working in her studio making illustrations for a new book. The day before the visit, Mr. Reese leads his students in a discussion to informally assess and, as necessary, sharpen their ability to develop incisive questions.

Mr. Reese: Let's make a list of questions to ask the author tomorrow. Recall what we know from her books, the video that we watched, and her biography, and think of questions that will give us additional information. Think of questions that cannot be answered in a word or two or whose answer can be easily found, such as "Where were you born?" Instead, I might ask, "What was your childhood like?" That would interest me. I'll write your questions on the whiteboard.

Jaden: Is it hard to write a book?

Mr. Reese: If the author says, "Yes," what would you ask her then?

Jaden: What makes it hard to write a book?

Mr. Reese: Yes, that will give us more information. Maybe you could just start with that question.

Rosa: But maybe she would say, "No!" Maybe it's easy to write a book.

Mr. Reese: Good point, Rosa. What do you suggest?

Rosa: Maybe asking, "What makes it harder or easier to write a book?"

Mr. Reese: What do you think of that, Jaden? Of Rosa's change to your question?

Jaden: It's okay. But it sounds better to say, "What makes it hard or easy *for you* to write a book?"

Mr. Reese: Yes, I agree. And Rosa seems to agree, because she's nodding her head. If you will allow me, I'd like to suggest a slight rephrasing of the question. What does everyone think of "What part of writing books is easy for you and what part is hard?" *(lots of nods)* Another good way to really understand something well is to ask follow-up questions. These questions use the answers from the first question to learn more, to dig a little deeper. If the author says that it is easy for her to come up with story ideas, I might ask, "Where do your best ideas come from?"

There are good opportunities for students to practice asking incisive questions when they work in pairs and small groups, help each other, interview each other, and interview family members.

Helping students develop parsing skills is critically important to counter the increasingly sophisticated ways that rumors, lies, and advertising are disguised as factual, objective information on the internet, on television, and in other media. Users of social media should put a sign by their computers: "Parse before you post!"

Evaluate

The purposes of an evaluation are to be better informed, to form an opinion, and/or to have the information necessary to make a decision, determination, or judgment. "It doesn't fit" is an evaluation. "It's the wrong part" is a judgment based on that evaluation. Evaluating consists of making a critical comparison of what is actual against certain criteria. The criteria can be straightforward and easy to determine objectively: "It can't cost more than ten dollars" or "The words have to be spelled correctly." They can also be complex and difficult to determine objectively: "It has to please everyone!" or "The answer must be thorough." These criteria require developing a set of subcriteria for what constitutes "pleasing" and "thoroughness."

Good evaluation thinking helps to mediate snap judgments and make judgments more intentional. It is the higher-order link between information and a determination, and it helps to minimize bias and maximize objectivity. Tests are formal evaluations. They are a tangible form of evaluative thinking, much like icons or symbols are a tangible form of representational thinking. Tests that are valid, are reliable, and provide useful information reflect advanced levels of evaluative thinking.

During a sports event, the referees or umpires are constantly evaluating the players' actions by weighing them against the rules (the criteria). Their primary evaluation criterion is whether a rule has been broken, but they also evaluate how much a rule has been broken. Not every infraction is serious enough to warrant a penalty, and some are so serious as to warrant a harsher than usual penalty. Evaluating the seriousness of an infraction uses criteria on a continuum from "apparently unintentional and minor" all the way to "intentional and dangerous." Referees also evaluate the condition of the playing field, the health of the players (particularly if there is an injury), and, in the case of soccer, how much time to add to the game after regulation time has expired. These evaluations are based on more subjective, flexible criteria than rules. Players and fans expect referees to make their evaluations quickly, accurately, consistently, and objectively. This is very difficult because human beings are not machines—which is why machines and technology are increasingly being used to verify or negate a ruling, assist referees in making accurate evaluations, or replace referees entirely. There are slow-motion videos from multiple angles, goal-line cameras, ball-tracking technology, and much more. The intent of this overly drawn-out sports analogy is to make the point that the accuracy of a decision, ruling, or judgment is wholly contingent on the quality of the evaluative thinking that went into it.

Effective evaluation thinking consists of careful attention to detail, knowing the criteria thoroughly, and applying the criteria objectively and fairly but also flexibly. At more advanced levels, evaluation thinking considers exceptions, unusual circumstances, the particular individuals involved, and other contextual factors.

There are many naturally occurring opportunities to help students strengthen these abilities. For example, a third-grade teacher offers her class the options of going outside for recess (even though it's raining lightly), playing in the gym, or continuing to work on projects in the classroom. She has the students form three groups based on their preferences, and she makes a three-column chart, one for each option. Each group gets a chance to say why their choice is better than the other choices, and the teacher writes a few key words in each column to capture their ideas. In the process, she scaffolds students' evaluation thinking skills and, at the end, states one additional pro and con for each choice to model more advanced evaluation thinking. Finally, the teacher brings the class back into one group, summarizes the information on the chart, and facilitates a vote.

Evaluating is an essential HOT skill, and although a common activity in schools, it is rarely considered an important skill for students to have. It is not often included as a student goal, addressed in curricula, or assessed, particularly for young learners. But students need many opportunities to practice developing evaluation criteria and applying them fairly and objectively. One effective way to do this is for students to evaluate each other's work, as well as their own. The following *Cognitivity* offers a method for peer evaluations that minimizes competitiveness and all but eliminates negative criticism and hurt feelings. The activity described on the following pages was preceded by three similar evaluation activities over the course of a month. Each activity was a little more complex than the previous one.

COGNITIVITY: MAKING MAPS

As part of a project on cartography, first-grade students work in small groups to make a map of the school. (Older preschoolers and kindergartners can make a map of the classroom, second graders can make a map of the neighborhood immediately around the school, and third graders can make a map of the

FIGURE 6
MAP EVALUATION FORM

Things are generally where they are supposed to be and nothing major is left out. *The map is accurate.*

Things on the map are orderly and neatly drawn. The shapes of things on the map have the same (or similar enough) shapes as the real things. *The map is easy to read and follow.*

Larger things are also larger on the map than things that are smaller. Things that are nearer to or farther from each other are the same way on the map. *The map is generally in proportion.*

broader community around the school.) Before they begin, the teacher facilitates a class discussion to develop a few criteria for making a good map. They come up with three categories of criteria: Is it accurate? Is it easy to read and follow? Is it in proportion? Based on these categories, the teacher develops an evaluation form for each student to complete, as shown in figure 6.

After Group 1 presents their map to the whole class, the other students fill out the evaluation form. They put a circle around the box for Group 1 if they believe the map met the criteria. They put a line through the box if they believe it does not meet the criteria. (When students become adept at this, the teacher adds a three-scale evaluation system in which students evaluate if they believe the criteria is met a little bit, mostly, or completely.) Following the presentations and evaluations from every group, the teacher collects the evaluation forms and shares the results with each group. The teacher helps each group figure out what they could do to improve their maps based on the evaluation results. Later in the day, or the next day, the groups are given the opportunity to redraw their maps, and the presentation and evaluation process is repeated.

Evaluating is different from judging, although they are often used interchangeably in everyday speech. A judgment is made at the end of an analysis by synthesizing the evaluations made during the course of the analysis, along with other factors and information (see "Analyze," pages 81–84, for more information). Examples of judgments are grades on report cards, a guilty or not guilty verdict from a jury, or a thumbs up or down from a movie critic.

Infer

Making inferences entails gleaning information that is indirectly related, implicit, or incomplete. The ability to infer appears to be innate. Preverbal eight-month-old babies can make simple inferences from basic visual clues (see chapter 6, page 91). Most four-year-olds can infer that Little Red Riding Hood is in danger from the wolf, although she does not seem to know it and it is not stated explicitly in the story (in most versions). We commonly infer how others feel based on how they look or act or from their voice tone, even when their words give a very different message. When our friends stop returning our messages, we infer that they are upset with us or that something has happened to them.

But inferring becomes a very advanced thinking skill when processing subtle, complex, ambiguous, or conflicting information. Spies or intelligence agents infer from bits of information found in photos, videos, documents, and written and spoken communications—all of which may or may not be accurate, relevant, or related to each other—to determine if there is imminent danger to the country, the nature of the danger, and who may be behind it.

Books are a great resource for promoting the development of students' inferential thinking. Teachers can ask students to say as many things as they can infer about the book just from carefully examining the information on the cover. Then, as they or the teacher reads the book, they answer questions that require inferential thinking, such as why a character did or said something unexpected, when and where the story takes place, what one character feels about another character, and what messages the author is sending through the story.

Here is an enjoyable *Cognitivity* to promote inferential thinking. Using a picture sentence, similar to the one below, students point to the picture and/or the word that is emphasized with each reading.

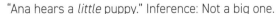

COGNITIVITY: SAME WORDS, DIFFERENT MEANINGS

The teacher reads the following sentences emphasizing the word in italics and leads a discussion about the different meanings they infer.

Ana hears a little puppy.

"*Ana* hears a little puppy." Inference: Do *you* hear it? Or, Khati doesn't hear it.

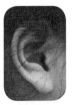

"Ana *hears* a little puppy." Inference: She can't see it.

"Ana hears a *little* puppy." Inference: Not a big one.

"Ana hears a little *puppy*." Inference: Not a full-grown dog, kitten, or other animal.

Then the teacher reviews a sentence similar to the one above (without pictures) demonstrating how emphasizing a particular word and using body language can change the inferred meaning of a sentence. For example, cupping one's ear when the word *hear* is emphasized and pretending to hold something small when *little* is emphasized. After students have experience with this activity, they work in small groups to make up a sentence and demonstrate to the class how verbally and physically emphasizing different words changes the inferred meaning of the sentence.

Shift Perspective

This is the ability to see things from another point of view. It encompasses both interpersonal and physical/spatial perspective taking. It is the basis of empathy when seeing another person's point of view and the basis of spatial acuity when visualizing physical objects and spaces. Psychologists shift perspectives to understand and connect with the people they are helping. Professional hockey players, among other athletes, can quickly visualize their location and movement trajectory on the ice, as well as those of their teammates and opposing players, including the players who are behind them. This gives them the ability to slip past defenders and very quickly and accurately pass or catch the puck. High-level shifting perspective thinking is behind those amazing "no-look" passes.

Taking the perspective of others involves the ability to collect and understand visual and verbal information about the person, read nonverbal cues, and accurately determine the feelings being expressed (deduce). Until recently, this ability has been viewed as something that is beyond the capacity of young "egocentric" children. However, we now know that even preverbal babies are capable of empathy in surprisingly sophisticated ways. Intuitively, it may seem that the ability to see things from another person's perspective is a more complex mental task than, say, visualizing a bird's-eye view of a room. However, for most young students, social-emotional perspective taking is easier than physical or cognitive perspective taking (Hamlin, Wynn, and Bloom 2007; Hamlin, Newman, and Wynn 2009). The reasons for this are discussed in chapter 6.

Characters in stories provide many good opportunities to help young students develop the ability to shift perspective. What would the story of Little Red Riding Hood sound like if told from the perspective of the grandmother or the wolf? *A Chair for My Mother* by Vera Williams is a heartwarming story in which a little girl expresses her concerns and hopes for her mother, who works long hours as a server after they lose everything in a house fire.

The previously described *Cognitivity,* Making Maps, on page 51, helps students develop the ability to shift perspective visually. To make the maps, they need to mentally transform large three-dimensional objects as viewed at ground level from the front to small two-dimensional shapes as they would look viewed from above.

Transfer

Transfer thinking, also called generalizing, is the ability to take a concept and adapt it to work successfully in a different context and/or for a different purpose. *Transferring* is the preferred term, as *generalizing* has a negative connotation, particularly when referring to people, as it also can mean assuming what is true of one or a few people in a group is true of every person in that same group.

Architects use transfer thinking regularly. Every structure they design is unique but uses features, styles, and techniques that, in nearly all cases, have been used before. One such technique, the architectural cantilever, allows for a large, heavy structure to overhang or thrust out without structural supports underneath. It was made famous by Frank Lloyd Wright in 1935 with his Fallingwater house, which features two large concrete balconies protruding from the external walls and over a waterfall. Now cantilevers are more commonly used to build bridges and to create roofs over sports stadiums, as they allow every spectator to have an unobstructed view of the field. Although all cantilevers use the same principles of physics, they often look very different from each other because architects are able to transfer the concept and make it work for various purposes and for many styles of architecture and types and sizes of structures.

One of the ways that transfer thinking is used by young learners is when they begin to realize that they have to behave differently in different places or under different circumstances. Most young students understand this to a degree, although somewhat instinctively and unconsciously. They naturally behave a bit differently outside on the playground than inside the classroom and differently at school than at home. But they have difficulty—as do many adults—when behavioral norms and expectations are unusual, ambiguous, arbitrary, or just unstated and unknown. Adults find it amusing (although parents can find it a little embarrassing) when children unintentionally violate an unstated social norm such as singing loudly in the supermarket or showing all the dinner guests their new Wonder Woman underpants. These events suddenly remind us that there are many such unstated social norms, which we just assume everyone knows.

In many cases, there are good reasons for particular behavioral norms, but they can be hard for a young person to understand. "Why can I take my shoes off

Whose Norms Are Normal?

While in most places in the United States children do not remove their shoes at school, in many countries students are required to remove their shoes before entering the school building. In some places they wear some type of indoor slipper, but in others they are just barefoot. Other school norms in the United States are not at all "normal" elsewhere. I was quite surprised by what I saw visiting elementary schools in an eastern European country. During the transition between classes, there were no prohibitions on running, yelling, or fighting in the hallways. The principal walked past two second graders physically fighting with each other, with barely a glance in their direction. The politicians of this country are somewhat infamous for throwing punches at each other during parliamentary sessions and on live TV news broadcasts. If students are not taught to use higher-order thinking during conflicts when they are young, some will never learn alternatives to physical violence.

On the other hand, classrooms in this country are more boisterous and lively than most classrooms in the United States, although they are calm compared to the hallways during transitions, and teachers keep enough control to prevent chaos. Students move about, argue passionately, shout out their ideas and opinions, and express their feelings and emotions, including affection for their teacher. At any given moment, somewhere in the school there are students dancing traditional dances or singing traditional music, which are integral to this country's culture. Perhaps classroom norms that encourage overt enthusiasm and enjoyment for school and learning and that incorporate music and dance would benefit many students and teachers in US classrooms.

at home but not at school?" "Why can I eat fried chicken with my fingers but not a grilled chicken breast?" The understanding and ability to act differently and appropriately in different environments is an early and basic step in the development of transferring. The teacher's role is to make these differences explicit and clear and help students to adapt. Students benefit from knowing the reasons for different expectations. Although it can be challenging for teachers to come up with simple explanations that young learners can understand, it is an ability that teachers can learn quickly with a bit of practice. Here is an example: "Because there are many, many more people at school than at home, there are some things we can't do at school that we can do at home." First explaining the overarching concept behind norms and then the reason for the norm helps students develop transfer thinking. "We keep our shoes on at school because if someone accidently stepped on your bare toes, which is likely to happen with so many people here, it would really hurt."

It is not realistic to expect that most young students can use transfer thinking without assistance, other than at a basic level; however, they are often expected to. What it means to be a good student and well behaved to a first-grade teacher may be quite different from what it means to a second-grade teacher, and it may have nothing to do with age-related expectations but all to do with each teacher's personality and teaching style. To successfully make the transition, students have to first understand that teachers have different expectations and then transfer their first-grade concept of "good student," with all the associated behaviors, and adjust it to the new context. A wise second-grade teacher understands that transferring is difficult but emergent for young students and makes her concept of "good" very clear from the first day of school. She supports students while they make the mental and behavioral transfer during the first weeks. In this way, she will prevent many problematic behaviors from developing and reduce students' anxiety while increasing their positive engagement in learning.

Creative Thinking Skills: The Sky's the Limit

To some people, creative thinking comes easily and naturally. Among them is a significant subgroup of people who are compelled to think creatively. They often have a very difficult time as students because typical school activities give them few outlets for their creativity. Creative thinking and creativity are often misunderstood as rarified skills that only a few possess. Perhaps this is because they are not typically used as an instructional strategy or taught directly. They are mistakenly considered extracurricular, such as the art classes or music lessons taken after school. But creative thinking is an essential and common life skill used every day, such as when generating ideas at a work meeting, imagining a kitchen remodel, adapting a recipe, making up a story to tell children, thinking of new theme ideas, transforming a dull mundane activity in a teacher's guide into an engaging and challenging one, and so on.

With guidance and practice, most people can think creatively with more intention for greater effect, at more advanced levels, more often, and in more situations. For example, conflicts and disagreements tend to get resolved either by someone winning and someone losing or by both sides reluctantly compromising. However, by using the creative thinking skill of reframing, the problem can often be resolved so that neither side loses or is forced to compromise. As with all thinking skills, creative thinking can be improved upon, expanded, and sharpened with appropriate instruction, support, and practice. Strategies and techniques for doing this are provided throughout the book.

Imagine

This is the core creative thinking skill. Imagining is necessary for all creative endeavors. Nonetheless, using one's imagination has negative connotations in some education programs, where it is associated with frivolous rather than "academic" activities. However, Albert Einstein, a man who obviously had an extraordinary amount of academic expertise, said, "Imagination is more important than knowledge" (Viereck 1929, 117). Many educators do not realize how important it is for students to have good imaginations and to use them often. Among other benefits, it helps them better understand nearly everything from word problems in math to abstract science concepts (such as how the earth looked millions of years before humans evolved) to challenging passages in a book they are reading.

An artist—whether a painter, sculptor, composer, or choreographer—creates something tangible from what was first in her imagination. People with strong imaginations are often drawn to the arts where they can express what they envision in their minds. Many of our most creative artists today did not do well in school because they had very few opportunities to use their imaginations and express themselves creatively. They were rarely able to show off their strengths and often felt stifled, frustrated, inept, and out of place.

Rather than relegating the activities that engage imaginative thinking to art, music, special occasions, or breaks from academic work, it is important to add creative elements to nearly every activity. This not only meets the needs of the young artists in your classroom, but it also helps those students not predisposed to using their imaginations to practice this important thinking skill.

In addition, there are many activities whose main purpose is to sharpen and expand imaginative thinking, some of which are quick and easy to implement, such as this *ThinkinGame.*

THINKINGAME: SHAPE SHIFTING

Sitting in a circle, students pass around a piece of stiff card stock in the shape of an equilateral triangle whose sides are about eight inches long. Each student holds it and says and shows what it could be, such as a hat, bib, mask, sign, slice of pizza, or other object. Students are encouraged, but not pressured, to come up with an original idea. Passing or delaying a turn is always an option. Each time the game is played, the shape is changed. Challenges are added as students become proficient, such as using two shapes at time. The game can also be played with objects such as a garlic press, a large wooden spoon, bacon tongs, a potato masher, a tennis or paddle ball racket, a small branch, or a large pine cone.

The following *Cognitivity* illustrates the facilitation of imaginative thinking skills from more basic to more advanced. Students are given a challenge to invent something. They can work in small groups or in pairs. The inventions can easily connect to any content area or can target particular abilities to practice or improve.

COGNITIVITY: INVENTORS INVENTING INVENTIONS

- Invent a new animal by combining parts of two different existing animals. (It can be made more complex by requiring that they describe the animal's character, habitat, diet, or other elements.)

- Invent a new musical instrument. It could be made up of parts of existing instruments or be something entirely original. Explain how it is played and demonstrate how it sounds.

- Invent a new country. Describe its history, language, food, music, geography, dress, and so on. Explain why it was only recently "discovered."

- Invent a new video game that will entertain as well as teach about a country, famous person, historical event, or science or math concept. Describe and explain the game in detail along with drawings. Create a storyboard that will show how the game changes as it progresses. Identify its strong points and potential problems or weaknesses.

Interpret/Synthesize

In general, interpretive thinking involves taking something that already exists and making it one's own. The expression "Put your own spin on it" captures the idea.

Because the word *interpret* has multiple meanings, it is important to understand its meaning as a thinking skill. It involves conscious and subconscious thinking. It is a creative thinking skill because the number and variety of interpretations are unlimited, and every person's interpretation is different and reflects each individual's unique sensibilities. Synthesizing is very similar. The essence of synthesizing is the idea that the whole is greater than the sum of its parts. Synthesizing thinking is like weaving a tapestry. There are many colorful threads (ideas, concepts, opinions, facts) that may have little or no meaning individually until they are woven (synthesized) into a pattern or a picture.

An example of basic interpretive/synthesizing thinking is taking a recipe and improving it, transforming it, or making it more to one's liking. Ideas may be pulled from other recipes, available ingredients, previous culinary experiences, or knowledge of how ingredients interact. Creativity is essential to interpretive/synthesizing thinking. Doubling the recipe is a logical thinking skill, and substituting honey for sugar employs (basic level) critical thinking. But "Dad's Deluxe, One-of-a-Kind, Best-in-the-World Pancakes" is interpretive/synthesizing thinking at its most delicious.

At a very advanced level, performing artists bring their own ideas, styles, and sensibilities to the piece they are performing. Our greatest performing artists often do not differ much from the very good ones in terms of skill or talent. They differ because of their ability to interpret pieces in ways that are assured and unique while being perfectly attuned to the music or, for actors, the characters. These interpretations feel so right that it's hard to imagine they could be done any other way or better. Actors draw on their knowledge base about the playwright and her intentions, the historical and political context of the plot, the characters, the setting, and previous performances. They critically reflect on the work, their feelings and ideas about it, and their own strengths and challenges in relation to it. They synthesize all of this information in unique and creative ways and embody it in their performances. They further reflect on their performances and make adjustments so that their unique interpretations are fully realized.

What are the implications of promoting this type of thinking with young learners? Most are not yet capable of thinking at this advanced level. But the foundation is set when students begin to gain proficiency in the previously described HOT skills that comprise logical, critical, and creative thinking.

Some students, particularly third graders, can start to combine HOT skills to accomplish a more complex task. Project-based learning in mixed-ability groups with ample time and assistance from teachers and parents will facilitate this. Projects naturally lend themselves to integrating and weaving content area learning and, being multifaceted and complex, to applying many different types of thinking skills. In addition, students use a combination of text, speech, drawings, models, videos, and photos to document their projects' process (see "Projects and Investigations," on pages 121–124, for more information).

The ability to interpret and synthesize, even at a basic level, requires training, support, and practice. One way to promote it is to ask students to express their feelings and opinions about significant events, books they read or that are read to them, a film or video that the class has watched, and experiences such as field trips. This should be done in addition to asking students to reflect critically. This way they will learn that there can be many equally valid interpretations and ways of synthesizing the experiences of any event. Teachers can then help students improve their interpretative thinking skills by expanding their vocabularies, asking them to support their opinions and feelings with specific examples, and helping them to be clear and succinct.

Induce/Theorize

Inductive thinking involves piecing together information to create something new, to come to a new or deeper understanding, or to make a prediction or hypothesis. Closely related to this is theoretical thinking, which involves connecting information to develop a concept (theory) that unites the information and explains how they are related. At advanced levels, inductive and theoretical thinking are both characterized by a desire to answer important questions and address critical problems. The level of inductive/theoretical thinking depends on the amount and complexity of the information that is used to develop a theory or create something. For example, composers use inductive thinking by drawing on their knowledge of musical structures and qualities—scales, keys, tonality, volume, harmonics, phrasing—to create a new piece of music. Lawyers employ inductive thinking when they use evidence to build a case. And thinkers from Plato (holistic education) to B. F. Skinner (behaviorism) to John Dewey (progressivism) to Howard Gardner (multiple intelligences) developed theories about the ways children learn and develop that have greatly influenced educational practices.

Inducing and deducing are like siblings with opposite personalities. Inducing involves combining or adding information, while deducing involves separating or eliminating information. But they live in the same house. Both can be applied to the same task and both have the same aim: to reach an informed conclusion or result. Activities that promote inductive thinking and theorizing are, unfortunately, too rare in schools. Asking young students to create a game using elements from the games they already know or to make up a story combining the characters and plots of two different stories are ways to promote the development of their inductive thinking skills. Teachers can promote theorizing by guiding discussions with students using questions that do not have definitive answers and then gradually increasing the complexity of the topics: "Why do people have pets?" "What is the difference between work and play?" "What does it mean to be smart or intelligent?" "Why are some people poor and some people rich?" "Why are there wars?"

In education, there are opposing theories about the best way to promote student learning and achievement. On one side are those who follow a data-centric theory and believe that uniform standards and expectations, benchmarks, measurable outcomes, copious testing, and accountability systems are the way to go. On the other side are educators who follow a learner-centric theory and believe that individualized goals and instructional strategies, informal classroom-based formative assessments, a positive classroom climate, meaningful and engaging curriculum, family partnerships, and so on are the best way. The proponents of both theories claim that the evidence (pieces of information) supports their theory of student achievement. However, each side is likely not developing theories from all the available information about student learning but are instead selectively finding the information that supports the theory they already subscribe to. In this case, they are not using inductive/theoretical thinking but LOT skills like identifying and organizing, and they are succumbing to a common thinking error called confirmation bias. Inductive/theoretical thinking is a creative thinking skill because the result or the theory is not fully known beforehand.

It is important that students eventually have some ability to theorize in an intellectually rigorous way. This may not be possible until young students are older, but teachers can lay the foundation by being explicit about what a theory is, what it means to theorize, and by encouraging nascent theorizing. Many young learners can theorize at a basic level, although they will likely need assistance and support to express themselves clearly and in sufficient detail.

The *ThinkinGame* Family Groups, described below, promotes simple inductive thinking and theorizing, requires no materials, and can easily be adapted for a broad age/ability range. This game is followed by a *SnapsHOT* of a problem-solving activity that requires inductive thinking.

THINKINGAME: FAMILY GROUPS

The teacher first explains the concept of families of things, starting with human families, and represents it graphically with a flow chart (a logical thinking skill), as illustrated in the top part of figure 7. Then she explains that the term *family groups* can be used to describe types of animals, such as insects, fish, and birds. With the students' input, she develops a Bird Family Groups chart, similar to the one shown in the lower part of figure 7.

The teacher then lists types of fish and sea mammals while the students try to identify the family groups to which they belong. She tells them that in addition to animals, other things that are related can be in the same family group or

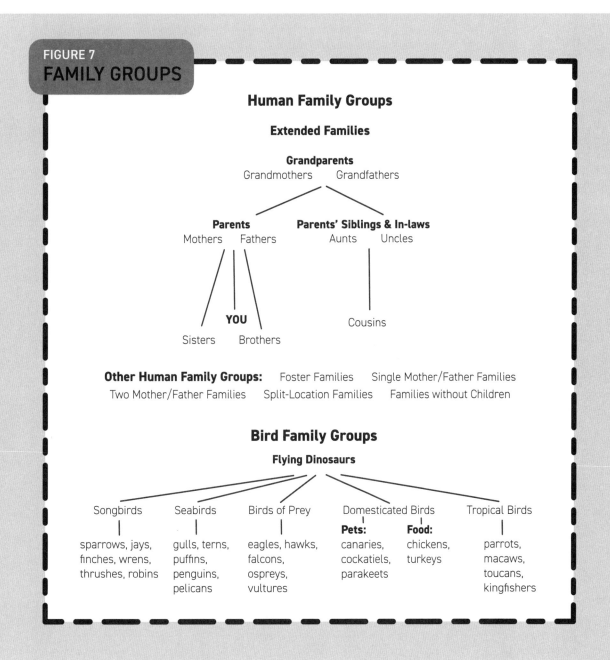

FIGURE 7
FAMILY GROUPS

Human Family Groups

Extended Families

Grandparents
Grandmothers   Grandfathers

Parents   **Parents' Siblings & In-laws**
Mothers   Fathers   Aunts   Uncles

YOU

Sisters   Brothers   Cousins

Other Human Family Groups: Foster Families   Single Mother/Father Families
Two Mother/Father Families   Split-Location Families   Families without Children

Bird Family Groups

Flying Dinosaurs

Songbirds   Seabirds   Birds of Prey   Domesticated Birds   Tropical Birds

sparrows, jays,   gulls, terns,   eagles, hawks,   **Pets:**   **Food:**   parrots,
finches, wrens,   puffins,   falcons,   canaries,   chickens,   macaws,
thrushes, robins penguins,   ospreys,   cockatiels,   turkeys   toucans,
                  pelicans   vultures   parakeets   kingfishers

category, and she challenges the students to name the family group for a set of items. For preschoolers, the items might be shirts, pants, dresses, hats, shoes, and so on. And, of course, the family group is "clothing" or "things that people wear." For kindergartners, the family groups can be more challenging, such as "jewelry," "forest animals," or "things people eat for breakfast." First graders can be further challenged with family groups, such as "things you can see at a construction site," "things that are loud," and "things that open and close." For second graders, family groups might include "things that melt," "things that smell good/bad," and "things that come in pairs." For third graders, "things that are found below the surface of the earth," "characters in books by Roald Dahl," and "things that are unfair."

As students become adept at the game, the categories can become more challenging to promote more advanced levels of theorizing, such as "things that people can't live without," "things that are ancient," "things that are micro-scopic," "excuses," and "parts of a piano." The last one is difficult because its main components are strings, keys, hammers, and pedals.

Another type of challenge is to include a mix of conceptual and tangible items in the list. "Things that you cannot hear" might include the voice of a giraffe, a baby crying in another city, silence, a television show with the volume on mute, and what someone is thinking. Of course, students can think up family groups and create lists to challenge their classmates.

Family Groups can also be played in the form of a game show, with teams that compete over time. Points can be won in several ways, such as determining the category before the other teams do, creating lists of items that stump other teams but are accurate, or some combination of the two.

The following *SnapsHOT* illustrates the value of inductive thinking for solving a problem and understanding a challenging concept. It is hands on, interactive, and appropriate for young learners. It starts with the teacher going through a process of changing a mundane and unchallenging sink-and-float activity to a more challenging and complex activity that, nonetheless, is misguided, unsuccessful, and does not involve higher-order thinking. Finally, she reframes her approach and changes it again to an intentional activity that promotes a number of HOT skills and is more successful in developing students' understanding of flotation.

SNAPSHOT: FLOAT YOUR BOAT

Flush with ideas from a recent workshop, Ms. Tamina sets up a new sink-and-float science work station in her kindergarten classroom. Although she has done this activity many times before, this time she is making it more scientific. She adds a tally sheet for students to record their findings and some new items to test along with all the items she had previously used: small pieces of newsprint paper, which float at first but eventually sink, and a small bottle that floats when empty and sinks when full of water.

Before students test each item, they complete the tally sheet, which has four columns. In the first column, they write the name or draw a picture of the object they will test. Then they put an *X* in one of the other three columns to indicate if they think it will float, sink, or do both. After testing, they put a checkmark in the column that indicates what actually occurred, as in figure 8 on page 66. Ms. Tamina asks individual students some probing questions when they are done, which is also a new addition to the activity. However, the responses surprise and concern her. While most students enjoy the activity, they all have difficulty hypothesizing (a type of inductive thinking) which items will sink or float or do both. Most are unable to explain the factors that make something float or sink. Tallying the findings was a tedious, meaningless process; their enjoyment is primarily from dropping things into water and retrieving them. Ms. Tamina puts away the activity at the end of the day but is determined to get it right.

After several days of researching on the internet, perusing some science books, and talking with friends and colleagues, Ms. Tamina tries a different approach. She realizes that abstract and complex concepts such as density, buoyancy, and displacement are at play, and if they cannot be made understandable to kindergartners, it is better to *not* do a sink-and-float activity because it can actually misinform them. Also, while she asked questions that required higher-order thinking, there was nothing in the activity, or that she did, to facilitate such thinking.

This time, Ms. Tamina starts with a short demonstration and discussion. "Here is a small plastic bottle filled with little pebbles and here is a big glass jar filled with . . . what?" The children shout, "Nothing!" "Actually, there is something in there: air. But air is very light, much lighter than water or pebbles. Which one is heavier, the bottle or the jar?" A few children feel them and say the jar is heavier. They put them on a balance scale, and the class sees that the jar is much heavier. "So, which one will float and which will sink? Or will they both sink? Or will they both float? I want you to hypothesize what will happen. Hypothesize means that you think carefully and try to predict or guess correctly

FIGURE 8
FLOAT YOUR BOAT

Object	Float	Sink	Both
FROK		X	
PINGPONG	✔	X	
PENCIL	✔	X	
SPUNS	✔		
CUP	✔	X	
penni		X	
KEY		X	

Name: Hannah B.

what will happen. Try to remember things that you have seen sink or float." Ms. Tamina records their answers after each one writes the word *sink* or *float* on a blue sticky note representing the small plastic bottle and on a pink sticky note for the glass jar. The answers are almost evenly split for each one. Then she invites two students to place them in the container of water. "So, the jar floats and the bottle sinks. What did we learn?" There is a lively discussion, after which Ms. Tamina says while demonstrating, "When we replace most of the air inside the jar with a rock, it will sink. And when we replace the pebbles with air in the bottle, it floats. Both our jar and the bottle can float because of their shape. They have empty space inside of them filled with air. In the same way, big ships can float on water although they are very, very heavy because they have a lot of empty space filled with air inside of them. Here are pictures of many different kinds of ships and boats. Let's look carefully at their shapes and determine how they each hold enough air so that they float even with people, engines, furniture, and other heavy objects on them.

"Now, work in small groups to make a boat that will float. You know it has to have a shape that holds air inside. You have heavy foil, pieces of wood, metal scraps, wire, and many other materials. You also have a set of stones. Your boat has to hold enough air to float with a stone on it. Maybe your group can even make one that will hold two or three or more stones and still float. You have resources, too. There are photos of different kinds of boats and ships, there are books that show the insides of ships, there are four buckets of water and the sink for testing your boats, and you can always ask for my help."

During the work, one group asks why a piece of wood floats when it's not shaped like a boat and has no place for air inside. Ms. Tamina interrupts the work of the class for a mini-lesson. "There is actually a lot of air inside a piece of wood, not in one big place in the middle, but in tiny pockets all throughout the inside of the wood. Stones have no pockets of air, so they sink. I will pass around a piece of wood, a stone, and this very strong magnifying glass. You will be able to see these little pockets in the wood but not in the stone."

In addition to promoting inductive thinking, the activity in this *SnapsHOT* promotes generative and imaginative thinking, transferring, and connecting causes and effects. The students (and the teacher) also engaged in problem solving.

Reframe

Shifting perspective is a critical thinking skill, but shifting perception, or reframing, is a creative thinking skill. When shifting perspective, the other perspective or perspectives are known. But reframing can involve any number of possible changes in perception.

One of the most effective ways that skilled mediators resolve problems is to reframe the nature of the conflict for their clients. Conflict resolution, a particular type of problem solving, is usually viewed as requiring the use of logical and critical thinking skills to reach a compromise, but it can be much more effective with the addition of creative thinking skills, particularly reframing. In the *SnapsHOT* below, a mediator works with the administrators of an elementary school and the parents of a child who want to enroll him in kindergarten in the fall.

SNAPSHOT: REFRAMING A PARENT/SCHOOL CONFLICT

Lorenzo's fifth birthday is one day after the eligibility date for kindergarten. The neighborhood school offers full-day kindergarten and has an excellent reputation as an arts magnet school. But the administrators are adhering strictly to the rule and reject Lorenzo's parents' request to test his readiness for kindergarten. Lorenzo's parents have enlisted the help of their sympathetic state house representative and a reporter from the local paper, both of whom are more than willing to shine a light on the "ridiculous inflexibility" of public schools. At this point, both sides agree to meet with a neutral mediator.

After separate discussions with the school staff and the parents, the mediator learns that the projected kindergarten enrollment is larger than usual, mostly because of many out-of-neighborhood transfers, which were approved at the district level. She also learns that Lorenzo's father was recently laid off from his construction job and is trying to start a painting business, and his mother might lose her job if she takes any more sick days.

The mediator is then able to help reframe the situation as an unfortunate but necessary action to protect the incoming students and their teachers from overcrowded classrooms, rather than a rejection of a child or a case of insensitive bureaucrats being "ridiculously inflexible." Furthermore, she helps reframe the parents' issue as a plea for help rather than an unreasonable demand. They can't afford to pay for another year of child care when the family income has dropped so dramatically. As a resolution, the school offers the support of their whole staff and the many community leaders with whom they have connections to help Lorenzo's parents find affordable, quality child care. They apologize for communicating so poorly and assure them they will be very happy and proud to have Lorenzo as a student in the school year that follows. Lorenzo's parents agree to tell the representative and the reporter that the situation is resolved, and they apologize for the problems they caused the school.

Reframing is one of the more sophisticated and complex HOT skills, so it is not a common thinking skill among young learners. Nonetheless, there are some students who are capable of reframing at a basic level. Also, when teachers use this skill themselves, students learn what it is and how it functions, which is an important first step in the process of acquiring it. There is an example of a teacher and a student reframing in the *SnapsHOT* Orange Is the New Green, on page 146. Below is another example of a student reframing, which catches his teacher by surprise.

SNAPSHOT: IT'S TIME TO PARTY

The day before spring break, Mr. Ahmadi's third graders are looking forward to the party planned for the last half hour of class. But from the opening moments of class, the students are excited and restless, and Mr. Ahmadi, who is a first-year teacher, can't seem to settle them down to focus on schoolwork. Finally, he says to the class, "If you keep this up, I will cancel the party! I am drawing five boxes on the board. Whenever anyone talks when they shouldn't or is not doing their work, I will put an *X* in one of the boxes. If all five boxes have an *X*, then the party is canceled."

While this seems to work for about ten minutes, it doesn't take long for all five boxes to have an *X*. After lunch, a grumpy group of third graders return to their seats. Immediately, Jonah raises his hand. "Mr. Ahmadi, it's not fair that we can't have the party because of a few kids who ruined it. Can't the rest of us have the party? We were good." Mr. Ahmadi replies, "No, because those were the conditions I set, and whatever we do or don't do, it has to be as a whole class." Again, Jonah raises his hand. "Okay, but can't we do something to get our party back? Do something good to you show we can be good and we should have the party?" After being rendered speechless for a few seconds, Mr. Ahmadi says, "Well, I guess we can try something. I will set the timer for twelve minutes. If everyone does their work and pays attention the whole time, then I will erase one of the boxes. If you are successful, then we can try it again for another twelve minutes. If you are able to erase all five boxes, then we will have the party." In the end, they *do* have the party.

Jonah reframed the situation from a loss and a big disappointment to an opportunity for redemption and a win. Although punishments and rewards are not the most effective strategies for managing students' behaviors, Mr. Ahmadi did learn that rewards generally work better than punishments. This is especially the case when students identify the reward they want because they will be motivated to earn it.

Generate

Generative thinking is used to develop a completely new and unique idea or product. It is imagining with a focus and with intentionality. Brainstorming is one common form of this type of thinking, when the goal is to generate many unique ideas quickly rather than generating one or two "good" ideas. Generating ideas is an important aspect of the problem-solving process: What might have caused the problem? What are some possible solutions?

When asked about his failure to get results after working for many months on developing a new type of battery, the prolific inventor Thomas Edison responded, "Results! Why, man, I have gotten a lot of results! I know several thousand things that won't work." (Dyer and Martin 1910, 616). Edison is communicating two important points in this statement. One is the value of persistence; if something doesn't work, come up with another idea and try again. The other is that generating many, many ideas to solve a problem or create something new is a normal and necessary part of the process. It took over two thousand attempts before Edison figured out a way to transfer electrical energy into heat energy strong enough to emit a bright light without burning up all the materials. The result was the electric light bulb.

There are two main circumstances in which teachers help students generate ideas. One is spontaneous and the other is planned. Generating ideas spontaneously occurs when solutions are needed to resolve a conflict or to solve an immediate problem. Planned activities that engage students' generative thinking include brainstorming possible places to go for a field trip, ideas about a topic as part of a KWL (Know, Want to Know, Learned) or similar activity, suggestions for project ideas related to a theme, and ideas about physical and scientific phenomena such as how airplanes fly, what makes the wind blow, or what happens to the sun at night. Asking students for their ideas about these complex but common phenomena, which many adults cannot explain accurately, gets them to think deeply and gives teachers insight into how they think. Their thinking skills can be challenged even further when several students who have differing ideas discuss and debate among themselves who is "correct." Of course, they may all be incorrect or only partially correct, which would require more teacher involvement.

The ability to generate good ideas—those that are relevant to the issue, realistic, positive, and likely to work—is an emergent skill in young students. The teacher's role is to help students become more proficient at generating good ideas by giving them many authentic opportunities to practice without judging their ideas. Students will learn what constitutes a good idea over time when they participate in many teacher-facilitated peer group discussions about the merits of various ideas. Teachers can facilitate these discussions by keeping students on track and asking incisive questions, which also models this type of thinking: "What materials do we already have that can be used for this project, and what materials will we need to get?" "What about this idea would be hard to do, and what would be easy to do?"

Conclusion

The ten higher-order thinking skills—five critical thinking and five creative thinking skills—give us the ability to question assumptions, look beyond surface appearances (which are often misleading), make informed decisions, have insights, solve complex problems, create original art and designs, develop new ideas, and so much more. Advanced HOT skills, honed over decades, are the tools of leaders, innovators, problem solvers, intellectuals, artists, scientists, and even some athletes. The major stars of professional basketball are different from the average professional basketball players (who are all exceptional athletes) because they excel at using higher-order thinking along with their physical acumen. Many of them are not taller, stronger, or faster than the more typical players; they just use more MOT and HOT skills and use them at more advanced levels. They use logical thinking before a game to determine how to exploit the other team's weaknesses and counter their strengths, particularly for the players they will guard and who will likely guard them. During the game, they use creative thinking to surprise their opponents with unexpected moves and use strategic thinking to second-guess what their opponents will do next, attempting to stay a step or two ahead of them—figuratively and literally!

While not everyone can achieve advanced levels of higher-order thinking, nearly everyone can develop the full array of HOT skills necessary to be effective in all spheres of life. Yet HOT skills are too rarely called upon in typical school lessons and assignments and are even more rarely systematically developed in students, particularly young students. This chapter provides the initial step for helping teachers remedy this problem: to understand the concepts and components of higher-order thinking.

Key Ideas from This Chapter

- Higher-order thinking involves the transformation of information and ideas and the creation of new information and ideas.

- Critical and creative thinking are the two categories of higher-order thinking.

- The critical thinking skills are the ability to parse, evaluate, infer, shift perspective, and transfer.

- Parsing is the ability to look beyond surface appearances, or what is evident, to find deeper, truer, or more accurate meanings.

- Evaluating involves associating and differentiating an action or item with criteria, such as a student's writing with five criteria: uses correct spelling, grammar, and punctuation; clearly expresses thoughts or ideas; and is organized logically. It can form the basis for a judgment: the paper is well written and gets an A. But evaluations can provide useful information without judgments.

- Inferring is the ability to gain insights from partial or nonexplicit information or from pieces of information that are indirectly related or where the relationship is obscure.

- Shifting perspective entails both interpersonal and physical perspectives. It is the ability to see things from another person's point of view and to visualize objects or spaces from various angles.

- Transfer thinking is used to take an idea from one context and apply it successfully in different contexts.

- The creative thinking skills are the ability to imagine, interpret/synthesize, induce/theorize, reframe, and generate.

- Imaginative thinking is an essential part of all other creative thinking skills. Students with active imaginations need many outlets to express their creativity.

- Interpreting/synthesizing entails taking something that exists and making it uniquely one's own. It is a creative thinking skill because there are nearly unlimited ways that something, such as a piece of music, a complex text like the Constitution, or the design of a house, can be interpreted and synthesized.

- Inductive/theoretical thinking involves developing a new idea or a deeper understanding of a concept by putting together pieces of existing information in unique ways. Darwin uncovered the concept of evolution after years of systematically observing wildlife around the world.

- Reframing is a change in perception such as coming to a different understanding of an idea than was previously held. After a long and candid discussion with a social worker, the teacher reframes his perception of his student from being challenging to having challenges and from needing discipline to needing support.

- Generating is the thinking most readily associated with creativity and inventing. It can be done quickly and superficially, as with brainstorming, or deliberately and deeply, as with writing a novel.

Questions for Discussion

- Which HOT skills are you particularly good at and which do you find challenging? Why?

- Do you have some students who show early signs of being adept at one or more HOT skill? How do they demonstrate it and how do you respond?

- In the *SnapsHOT* It's Time to Party, the strategy for managing an excited group of students was reframed from punishing misbehavior to rewarding good behavior. What are other ways it could have been reframed?

- The ability to parse is an increasingly important thinking skill because information overload makes it ever more difficult to distinguish between what is important or trivial and what is fact or fiction. What are some challenges your students face that require parsing skills to deal with effectively? How can young learners start to develop or improve their parsing skills? 🧠

Key Thinking Processes:
Common Tasks, Complex Thinking

Choosing and making decisions, solving problems, planning and strategizing, and analyzing are the four key thinking processes, each of which involves the use of a variety of LOT, MOT, and HOT skills. These four processes encompass most of our daily mental activity, and each can be done quickly or methodically and at levels ranging from very basic to very advanced. Young learners are in the course of developing the skills that comprise these thinking processes and are gradually learning to engage in them more deliberately. Teachers can assist and support these efforts by naming the processes (and the thinking skills involved) when they and their students engage in them and by explaining the steps involved in the processes while guiding students through them.

These thinking processes are not typically a significant part of the curriculum for young learners, and when they are, they tend to involve activities that mostly engage students' LOT and MOT skills, and occasionally some HOT skills at a basic level. However, when a range of critical and creative thinking skills at the most advanced levels of students' capabilities are used to solve problems, make decisions, plan, and analyze, the processes are more thorough and the outcomes more effective and powerful. This puts the onus on teachers to develop activities that give students practice using these thinking processes in ways that engage and develop their HOT skills. Examples of such activities are provided in this chapter.

Choose/Make Decisions

Identifying (a LOT skill) and any or all of the logical thinking skills (MOT skills) are involved in making a choice or decision. Very complex decisions require advanced critical thinking skills, particularly evaluating. One type of decision made based on evaluations are judgments: Guilty or not guilty? A grade of A or B+? Thumbs up or thumbs down?

Choosing is a simple, brief form of decision making. The differences between them are subtle and the line is fuzzy; in common usage, the terms are interchangeable. Choosing a life partner is not simple, and deciding what to wear is not complex—at least it shouldn't be! For the purpose of understanding decision making in the context of teaching and learning, choosing is defined as a type of decision that has very few factors (variables) to consider and an outcome that is not of great consequence. It isn't a tragedy when the flight attendant's response to your choice of the chicken over the beef is "Sorry, we just ran out of chicken." (However, it is a mystery why this is always the response!)

Decision making, then, is a more formal, objective process, or it should be, as it involves multiple variables to consider, some of which are complex, and a consequential outcome. Sometimes a carefully made decision turns out badly, and sometimes people get lucky and a hastily made decision turns out well. But in most cases, a well-considered decision turns out badly because it was based on incomplete or inaccurate information or an unforeseen event occurred, not because the process was faulty. And, certainly, relying on luck is never a good idea.

So decisions should be made based on the best available evidence and information, careful evaluations of the options and pros and cons, and the potential consequences of the decision (connecting causes and effects). But even the most deliberated decision should be made with the understanding that it might be wrong and mid-course corrections may be needed, if they are possible.

Making good decisions is a key element of school and life success: For older students, on any given day, deciding whether, when, and for how long to play a video game, practice the cello, play basketball in the neighborhood, study, watch a movie, or read a book may not feel consequential, but the impact of these daily decisions made over a period of years *will* be significant. Making good decisions as a student sets the stage for making good decisions later in life as adults, including very consequential ones such as choosing which career to pursue, where to live, and who to marry. Giving young learners many opportunities to make acceptable, age-appropriate choices is a great way to start developing their decision-making skills. Chapter 9 has a section on choices (pages 146–148) with ideas to promote various types and levels of decision making. There are many natural opportunities throughout the day for students to make choices and practice decision making. With so much to do, teachers sometimes fail to take full advantage of these opportunities because they take a bit more time. There are also many ways to build more formal decision making into planned curriculum activities that are not costly in terms of time and resources. Students need opportunities and support to practice using HOT skills when making decisions.

Developing group decision-making skills is also important. Here is a *Cognitivity* designed specifically for young learners to make a group decision by voting. It is an extension of the *Cognitivity* Making Maps, on page 51.

COGNITIVITY: MAY THE BEST MAP WIN

While still in their small groups, each student in turn stands and briefly makes the case for why their map is the best. For some students, the teacher will likely need to give them some prompts and ask a few questions or make a few comments about the quality of the map based on the criteria they developed earlier in the mapmaking process. Then each group stands in turn. While a group is standing, all the other students who are sitting down either vote for that group's map by raising their hands or hold their vote for another group. This process ensures that students cannot vote for their own map. To keep themselves from voting more than once, they put a sticky dot on the palms of their hands immediately after they vote. The teacher can readily see if a student votes twice (accidentally, of course). The teacher tallies the votes, and the winning group receives appreciation and applause. Then a few willing students who are not in the winning group but voted for it are invited to say why it is a good map. Students in the winning group respond to questions about their process and their map. The map is posted on the wall or included in a documentation display about cartography and/or decision making.

For preschoolers or for groups of students for whom this voting process is too difficult, the discussions can be curtailed, teacher led, or eliminated. Also, the strategy for avoiding voting more than once can be made more concrete by having students fold their arms or hold a book after they vote.

Solve Problems

Whether the problem is simple or complex, effective problem solving involves the same set of thinking skills in the same sequence.

1. Identify (a LOT skill) the problem and find out as much as possible about the context and cause(s).

2. Examine the information to deduce (a logical thinking MOT skill) probable cause(s) of the problem (connect causes and effects, a logical thinking MOT skill).

3. Generate ideas of possible solutions (a creative thinking HOT skill).

4. Determine the criteria for what constitutes a good solution (characterize, a logical thinking MOT skill).

5. Evaluate the merits of the solutions based on the criteria (a critical thinking HOT skill).

6. Evaluate the effectiveness of the chosen solution based on the outcome. If the problem was solved, what was learned that could apply to similar problems in the future (transfer, a critical thinking HOT skill)?

7. Restart the problem-solving process if the problem was partially solved, not solved, or made worse.

This is, of course, a broad, generic description of the problem-solving process. Each of the seven steps can be broken down into many subtasks. Some of the steps may be quite difficult and time consuming, particularly the first step. Getting accurate and complete information about the problem is critically important. (For a more thorough treatment of problem solving in the context of teaching young children, see *Practical Solutions to Practically Every Problem: The Survival Guide for Early Childhood Professionals* [Saifer 2017].)

Customer service reps, technical support specialists, and consultants use problem-solving thinking extensively in their work. When we call customer service or technical support for a computer problem, the technician starts by asking a set of questions to identify the problem (step 1). She then proceeds to go through the next four steps, mostly to herself, to resolve the problem. Unfortunately, she isn't there for steps 6 and 7. When the problem reoccurs three days later, hopefully the computer is still under warranty!

Conflict resolution is a particular type of problem solving. As conflicts among students are common, there are many opportunities for teachers to develop their problem-solving skills. Rather than viewing conflicts as a distraction or as something students need to solve themselves, teachers should use them as teaching and learning opportunities.

Engaging in problem solving often and with many different types of problems is a key teaching and learning strategy for developing HOT skills because so many different thinking skills are used. Problems can be small and quickly resolved when teachers pose certain questions: "How can we fairly choose who will go first?" Or they can be large and complex: "What can we do so that the new families and children from northern Africa coming into our school feel welcomed?" The *SnapsHOT* Go with the Flow, on page 159, is an example of a teacher helping a preschooler solve a problem.

Plan/Strategize

Planning is a basic form of strategizing, and strategizing is a more intentional and complex form of planning. Strategizing also implies planning to achieve a specific outcome or in response to the actions of another person. In relation to strategizing, planning involves using more LOT skills (organizing and identifying) and logical thinking skills (the sequencing skill of prioritizing) than it does conceptual HOT skills.

Planning

Everyone plans often and regularly, although sometimes not as effectively as they could for the task at hand. While it's almost always a mistake to go to the store without a shopping list, only 44 percent of shoppers bring one (Food Marketing Institute 2016). Planning includes both students' planning and teachers' planning. Students learn a great deal when teachers think aloud about their planning and invite them to participate. This can be done informally and formally. When a teacher talks about planning a field trip, for example, she can solicit students' ideas and invite their feedback throughout the planning process, which may take several days. Planning something complex, such as a field trip, involves using several HOT skills: generating ideas for where to go, evaluating options, calculating costs and timing, and, of course, the thinking process of making decisions. Naming the thinking skills when planning with students helps make those skills visible and defined: "Let's do some higher-order thinking and generate even more ideas."

Informal opportunities to explain plans often occur naturally and spontaneously. Teacher Emma says the following to her preschoolers during morning circle:

> Yesterday, we planned to go for a walk to the park today, but it is raining hard and is very windy. So I think we should change our plans. I can think of three options: we can go for a shorter walk, we can reschedule our walk, or we can do both. Can

anyone think of another option? Let's evaluate the options and make a group decision.

Students also have many natural opportunities to plan, although teachers often need to provide some coaxing and assistance. Preschool and kindergarten teachers can review the daily schedule each morning and discuss any deviations. They can ask their students questions like "What do you plan to do in the art area?" and "What are your plans for spring break?" Second- and third-grade teachers help their students sharpen their emerging ability to self-plan as students begin to develop some basic planning skills. They ask their students questions like "How do you plan to finish the project by Friday?" and "If we want to raise money to purchase more tablet computers, what is our plan?"

Strategizing

Strategizing entails relatively advanced levels of the LOT skill of identifying; the MOT skills of sequencing (prioritizing) and connecting causes and effects; the HOT skills of evaluating, inferring, imagining, and generating ideas; and the thinking process of deciding.

A good illustration of this is how President Lyndon Johnson, a master political strategist, convinced Congress to authorize and fund the Head Start program in 1964. Shortly after he became president (after John F. Kennedy was assassinated), he declared a War on Poverty, with Head Start as one means for achieving that goal. It was just one program in a larger piece of antipoverty legislation that funded many new programs, including Volunteers in Service to America (VISTA). In those days, politicians from either party would face criticism for opposing a program for young children from poor families who, unlike their parents, were viewed as the "deserving poor" because they were in circumstances beyond their control. Johnson knew this would make it difficult for many members of the House and Senate to vote against the bill, although most opposed it. One strategic move was to keep the Head Start program relatively modest. It started as an eight-week, half-day summer program and targeted just the poorest counties in each state. This kept the funding amount low enough to deflect opposition because of its cost. First Lady Lady Bird Johnson, who was a persuasive speaker but soft-spoken and gentle, took a leading role in lobbying for Head Start. She provided a strategically smart counterpoint to her husband's gruffness and behind-the-scenes hard-nosed lobbying. These are just some of the strategies that President Johnson used to make Head Start a reality.

The essence of strategizing in competitive situations is to think several steps ahead of one's opponent. President Johnson was able to determine what others

were thinking and feeling (infer, shift perspective) to predict the opposing arguments (induce) as well as the activities and ideas that they would likely support.
He then used that information to develop a program and a process that would be
difficult for them to oppose (generate ideas, evaluate), embedded it among less
popular programs, and moved his antipoverty agenda forward.

Can young learners strategize? Yes, and they do it more often than adults realize. However, they have difficulty strategizing more than one or two steps ahead
or counter-strategizing, and they tend to do it reactively more than intentionally.
For example, five-year-old Luca is rebuffed by a group of classmates on the playground during recess. He strategizes to bring in a toy from home the next day that
he believes the other children will want to play with, which he thinks will lead
them to include him. He chooses a toy that is small enough to fit in his pocket so it
will be inconspicuous until recess. While Luca is able to strategize in two ways to
achieve his goal, he is unable to think far enough ahead to consider other options
if the toy won't be attractive to his classmates or if the playground monitor will
catch him and disapprove. It is more common to see children strategize in social
and interpersonal situations than in academic pursuits, in large part because few
school-based activities specifically call on strategic thinking. Outside of social situations, young learners' strategic thinking tends to be relegated to board games and
certain video games. Unfortunately, strategic thinking and other thinking skills
developed in these pursuits do not appear to transfer to academic and intellectual
activities (Burgoyne et al. 2016; Sala and Gobet 2016).

Analyze

Analyzing, also called critical analysis, involves an in-depth examination of something (such as event, concept, theory, text, or work of art) in order to fully understand it. The analysis may result in an interpretation or evaluation of it. Sometimes
the goal of an analysis is to have accurate information for improving it in some
way. Analyzing involves the use of many HOT skills and a few LOT skills.

In the case of movie reviews, critics identify plot elements and describe them
(LOT skills). They evaluate (a critical thinking skill) many elements of the film,
such as the quality of the story, the acting, and the cinematography. The evaluation criteria may be other movies that excel at these elements or the critic's own
standards. In some cases, they need to infer (a critical thinking skill) the intentions of the screenwriter or filmmaker. They make sure that these evaluations,
which could also be called opinions, are well supported by sound arguments
(associate/differentiate thinking and connecting causes and effects). In some
cases, they parse meanings (a critical thinking skill) from the film that may not

have been intended by the filmmaker or evident to the typical viewer. These may be positive or negative. A film that looks similar to other films may be derivative and unoriginal, an homage and loving tribute to the genre, or a creative update. They synthesize all this information (a creative thinking skill) to make a final judgment: thumbs up or thumbs down!

In addition to movie critics, essayists, op-ed columnists, television commentators, researchers, academics, book reviewers, lawyers, and judges, among other professionals, use critical analysis extensively. Sometimes analyzing is done with a very entertaining and biting wit, as in the case of the early-twentieth-century writers H. L. Mencken and Will Rogers and contemporary commentators such as Bill Maher and Stephen Colbert.

There are other types of analyses in addition to critical analysis: systems analysis, social-cultural analysis, behavioral analysis, structural analysis, content analysis, data analysis, and many more. Intrapersonal analysis is often referred to as critical reflection. While reflection (remembering, recalling) is a LOT skill, critical reflection, as with other forms of analyses, involves the use of HOT skills. Critical reflection is a self-analysis of events or actions that are recalled. With young learners, critical reflection primarily entails exploring the reasons for their feelings, opinions, or behaviors. This could involve trying to determine the reasons for feeling afraid of the dark or why the bridge they made in the sandbox keeps collapsing. For older students, it could involve trying to determine why they like a book.

The following *SnapsHOT* is an example of analyzing in the form of a critical reflection. The teacher is attempting to help his students do basic critical reflection when responding to "why" questions. The two examples of critical reflection in this *SnapsHOT* illustrate the teacher's advanced level of analytical thinking and the students' nascent and emergent level of analytical thinking.

SNAPSHOT: WHY IT'S HARD TO EXPLAIN WHY

Near the end of the day, Mr. Ortiz asks his kindergarten students to think about everything they did during the day. He then invites several students to name the activity they liked the most (recalling, a LOT skill, and evaluating, a HOT skill but at a basic level). This is something that nearly all the students do well. However, when he asks the question "Why did you like the activity?" which requires more advanced levels of critical thinking and some creative thinking (inducing/

theorizing), the responses are brief, vague, and general, if there is a response at all. Although Mr. Ortiz knows his students' ability to analyze is emergent, he wants to learn ways he can support and nurture its development.

Fortunately, Mr. Ortiz's critical analysis skills are strong. Later that day, he thinks about why his students have so much trouble expressing the reasons for their choices (shifting perspective). While reading an article on critical reflection, he is reminded that it first requires the ability to carefully and thoroughly review what occurred. But he had only required his students to name the activity—"going to the gym" or "the movie about the planets." So Mr. Ortiz generates the idea of asking them to describe the activity and scaffolding their thinking, as necessary, by slowing it down and expanding it through questions and brief discussions. He will help them describe the activity in as much detail as they can and, for now, stop asking "why" questions. (This is an example of how helping students use LOT skills at more advanced levels can scaffold the development of HOT skills.) When he implements this idea, he discovers that he can often determine why a student likes an activity by the aspects of it they choose to highlight and from changes in their voice tone and body language (shifting perspective). After a few more weeks of students' practicing to describe events in detail, Mr. Ortiz helps them identify the elements of their descriptions that indicate or infer (a HOT skill) why they liked it. They do a little better, but their responses are still brief and rudimentary and less detailed and expressive than their descriptions.

Analyzing is often more effective when the perspectives of others are added, particularly people with expertise and strong critical thinking skills. Because it is difficult to "see the picture from within the frame," critical self-evaluation has its limitations. When Mr. Ortiz shares his story with a more experienced friend and colleague, Elena, he invites her to observe him in his classroom. Elena is able to see that the students lack the vocabulary related to describing complex or nuanced feelings (or, perhaps, they do not know how to use the words in that context), words such as *satisfied, improved, capable, understood, fulfilled, excited, fascinated, unique, proud,* or *meaningful.* She suggests that Mr. Ortiz give them "lead-ins" such as "I liked it because it gave me . . ." "I liked it because I was able to . . ." "I liked it because it was the most . . ." She also suggests that Mr. Ortiz model vocabulary by always taking a turn at the end to describe the activity that he liked the best and explain why. After Mr. Ortiz employed these strategies over a two-month period, slowly, a little more than half the students were able to explain why they like something relatively clearly, logically, and in sufficient detail for their age.

Mr. Ortiz is admirable in his persistence and should be proud of the results of his labors, even if he was assisted a little by the rapid maturity of language skills that occurs between the ages of five and six.

Conclusion

There are several factors that apply to all four thinking processes and help ensure they will be informed with higher-order thinking:

- The information upon which plans and decisions are made, problems are solved, and analyses conducted is relevant, unbiased, complete, and accurate. Different strategies are required to help a student who is struggling to learn to read, depending on the cause of the problem. Is it due to a learning disability, uncorrected low vision, difficulty concentrating, lack of opportunities to practice, not being developmentally ready, or some combination of factors?

- The purpose of the process is clear and authentic. An analysis that is trivial or just an empty academic exercise does not challenge students to use HOT skills to their full potential, or at all, and therefore does not promote their development.

- While perfection may be the enemy of good, convention is the enemy of excellence. Teachers cannot expect students to challenge themselves with advanced higher-order thinking (for them) and strive for excellence if the problems they are asked to solve and the decisions they are asked to make are trivial or mundane.

- These processes are teaching and learning activities. Mistakes are not problems, they are learning opportunities.

The four key thinking processes encompass most of the kinds of thinking we do on a daily basis. They are common but important, and too often they are not done effectively because HOT skills are not used to the extent they could be. In schools, content can be taught through tasks that engage these thinking processes, giving students many opportunities to practice and hone them, and giving teachers many opportunities to develop students' abilities to do them effectively. Imagine how much better we all would be at making difficult decisions and solving thorny problems, how much more efficient and effective we would be at planning and strategizing, and how much better-informed and wiser we would be with the ability to analyze complex information, if these processes had been systematically nurtured in us from preschool through high school.

Key Ideas from This Chapter

- The four key thinking processes are choosing/making decisions, solving problems, planning/strategizing, and analyzing.

- Thinking processes involve the use of a variety of LOT, MOT, and, when done well, HOT skills. HOT skills are not often called upon in typical curricular activities that use these processes, particularly with young learners; however, when critical and creative thinking are applied to thinking processes, they are more effective.

- Choosing/making decisions: Making good decisions is a critically important skill for success in school and in life. This includes group decisions as well as individual decisions. Students need many opportunities to practice making a wide variety of decisions and assistance in applying HOT skills to the process.

- Solving problems: Many problems can be addressed using a similar process that begins with gathering information, proceeds to generating ideas for solutions, and ends with evaluating the results of the chosen solution. Teachers can offer students many types of problems to solve: naturally occurring problems, such as social conflicts, and curricula-based problems, such as how to make a boat that will float holding a stone, as in the *SnapsHOT* Float Your Boat, on pages 65–67.

- Planning/strategizing: Students can learn a great deal when teachers make their plans and planning processes explicit. Strategizing is typically a more intentional and complex form of planning, but it also implies planning to achieve a specific outcome. Young students are capable of basic strategizing, but it tends to be intuitive rather than deliberate and involves only one or two steps.

- Analyzing: This is the process of examining something closely and methodically to understand it well. In some cases, the analysis is done for a purpose, such as to critique a movie, as part of an investigation into a scandal, or to determine if a book is suitable for second graders. Critical reflection is a form of self-analysis, in which events are recalled and examined in order to understand one's own behaviors or actions. Often the purpose is to make improvements to be more effective in the future.

- Students need many opportunities to practice these thinking processes using HOT skills.

Questions for Discussion

- Recall a good decision that you made and a poor decision. Reflect critically on the factors that contributed to making the good decision and the poor decision. What lessons could you draw from these reflections to help students learn to make good decisions?

- What types of problems do your students deal with on a regular basis? What types of curriculum-based problems do you challenge them with? Take one example of a problem and determine if it engages students' HOT skills. Which HOT skills does it engage and at what level of challenge in relation to students' abilities? How can the activity be amended to engage more HOT skills and/or more advanced levels of higher-order thinking?

- Many board games and video games involve strategizing in order to win. This typically requires thinking two or three steps ahead (induce, deduce and/or infer) and second-guessing what an opponent will do next (shifting perspective). What are some ways that curriculum-based activities can be designed to promote these same HOT skills and the thinking process of strategizing? How can board games be modified (or created) to teach content while still challenging students to strategize?

- In the *SnapsHOT* Why It's Hard to Explain Why, on pages 82–83, the teacher scaffolds his kindergartners' ability to reflect critically (a type of analysis) and articulate the reasons for their feelings. He gives them cues, helps them with vocabulary, and models ways to do it. What are some other strategies he can use to help his students reflect critically? How can these strategies be used to help students analyze stories and events?

The Importance and Function of HOT Skills:

More Innovation, Less Imitation

In this chapter, I make the case that the way children think is not much different from the way adults think and that certain HOT skills are innate in human beings, as can be seen even in the behaviors of preverbal infants. These ideas have important implications for how we raise and teach our children. Because we haven't known until recently that very young children, even infants, are capable of higher-order thinking, we haven't looked for it, recognized it when it was there, or provided opportunities for it to be expressed, nurtured, and developed.

Activities and tasks that require students to use higher-order thinking develop their ability to think flexibly, deeply, and lucidly, which are the abilities they need to be successful academically and in life. Knowing many ways to think critically, creatively, and logically is necessary for learning complex content and processing new information. According to developmental psychologist Alison Gopnik (2016b), new forms of teaching, with an emphasis on creativity, are needed to ensure that students will be adequately prepared for the demands of the information age:

Studies show that explicit instruction . . . can be limiting. When children think they are being taught, they are much more likely to simply reproduce what the adult does, instead of creating something new. . . . As a result, the kind of teaching that comes with schools . . . pushes children toward imitation and away from innovation. . . . But the new information economy, as opposed to the older industrial one, demands more innovation and less imitation, more creativity and less conformity.

Why We Need a Little LOT and a Lot of HOT Teaching

The LOT teaching methods that predominate in schools are not effective. Only 37 percent of twelfth graders are proficient or better in reading, 25 percent in math, and 22 percent in science (National Center for Education Statistics 2016). The majority of American middle and high school students cannot distinguish fake news from real news or sponsored and biased sources from neutral and reliable sources (Wineburg et al. 2016).

LOT teaching methods predominate in preschools as well. It is not unusual to see an early childhood program with a reputation for excellence, attractive environments, caring teachers, small class sizes, mixed-age groupings, and a wide variety of engaging materials for the children, but where nearly all of the dialogue between teachers and students is simplistic. In an opening group meeting, the teacher asked the students to name vegetables as she pulled them, one at a time, from a bag. She was proud of the fact that she had real vegetables, some of which had come from a farm the class had recently visited. She felt successful because the students were engaged in the activity. But she only asked one question over and over: "What vegetable is this?" And she missed many opportunities to promote HOT skills. Early on in the activity, the teacher pulled a green bell pepper from the bag, whereupon most of the children shouted, "Pepper!" in response to her question. Later in the activity, she pulled a long red chili pepper from the bag, and again, most of the children shouted, "Pepper!" At that point, she could have shown both peppers and asked questions such as "What is it about these two very different-looking vegetables that tells you they are both peppers?" "How are they different and how are they the same?" "Have you seen another pepper that looks different from either of these?" "What does it look like?" Each of these questions would undoubtedly lead to a short discussion in which the teacher could help children hone their higher-order and logical thinking skills.

LOT teaching methods may actually interfere with the development of HOT skills and hinder the development of flexible thinking. For example, when a student is taught only algorithms for solving math problems (such as borrowing and carrying) and she almost always gets the correct answer, she will have little motivation to learn why and how the algorithms work or to learn alternative ways to solve math problems. And as she is "successful," her teacher may feel there is no need to teach anything beyond algorithms. But without the understanding that comes when higher-order teaching techniques are used, she will not be able to apply her knowledge to other contexts or to solve math problems mentally or when they are presented in unfamiliar formats (transfer thinking).

The ability to effectively use a wide array of HOT skills gives students flexibility in their thinking. Having gained a thorough understanding of a given topic and having transfer thinking and other HOT skills, they can apply what they have learned across a range of situations, contexts, and content areas. We now know that young students have the capacity to think in complex ways (Robson 2012; Siegler and Alibali 2005). We also know that when teachers intentionally develop their students' HOT skills, the students learn basic academic skills and knowledge better than when teachers focus only on basic skills. This holds true for all ages and grade levels, for students with disabilities, and for students from low-income families (Higgins et al. 2005). Unfortunately, students with disabilities and those from low-income families are much less likely to be taught higher-order thinking skills than their typically developing and wealthier peers (Noguera, Darling-Hammond, and Friedlaender 2015; Pianta et al. 2007).

New Thinking about Children's Thinking

Many of us were taught in our child development classes that young children, older children, adolescents, and adults think very differently from one another. We learned that the development of thinking occurs in stages and that each stage represents a significant shift in the nature, quality, and accuracy of a person's thinking ability. But the development of thinking, particularly higher-order thinking, is more like a continuum than a series of distinct states, more like riding an elevator between the first floor and the top floor than walking up the stairs and resting at each landing. Age-related differences in thinking are due to the differences in the number of experiences people have had and the brain's increasing capacity to hold, retrieve, modulate, and process information (that is, until old age when, for many but not all, it steadily declines).

While young children clearly hold many misconceptions and often use faulty logic, the same can be said about nearly all adults. The Nobel laureate economist Daniel Kahneman wrote the book-length treatise *Thinking, Fast and Slow* (2011), explaining the many ways that adults' thinking is often biased, distorted, and faulty. For example, a cognitively competent adult would not buy a lottery ticket, as there is almost a zero chance of winning. (Wanting to make a donation to the lottery fund is the only defensible reason to play.) For the multistate lotteries, the chances of winning are about 250 million to one, or a 0.000000004 percent chance. Yet in 2014, about half of all Americans living in the forty-three states with lotteries played them multiple times, and each person spent an average of $300, which collectively added up to $70 billion (Thomson 2015).

Just as children and adults share some unfortunate similarities in faulty thinking, they also share some fortunate similarities in higher-order thinking. All the types of HOT skills that adults possess, even those used by our most advanced thinkers, from theoretical physicists to poets, very young children also possess, although sometimes in an unsophisticated, tenuous, and emergent form.

Cognitive psychologist Daniel Willingham (2007, 10) writes, "Critical thinking is not a set of skills that can be deployed at any time, in any context. It is a type of thought that even three-year-olds can engage in—and even trained scientists can fail in. And it is very much dependent on domain knowledge and practice." What is domain (content) knowledge for a three-year-old? It includes very basic knowledge in the language domain and the rapid development of vocabulary and correct grammar and syntax through observation, listening, experimentation, and trial and error. Three-year-olds are also honing their social relations domain knowledge and starting to play collaboratively with other children. And in the domain of physics, they are improving their understanding and ability to manage the physical properties of objects, such as their shape, weight, hardness, fragility, and much more. So the activities of a three-year-old and a scientist are not all that different. They both use critical-thinking skills with intentionality to gain new knowledge through observation and experimentation, building on what they already know. The difference is in the level of complexity and sophistication of the content.

Daniel Kahneman (2011, 11) equates the brilliant, lightning-fast thinking of high-level experts, which he calls "expert intuition," with the thinking of toddlers learning to talk:

> We are not surprised when a two-year-old looks at a dog and says, "Doggie!" because we are used to the miracle of children learning to recognize and name things. . . . The miracles of expert intuition have the same character. Valid intuitions develop when experts have learned to recognize familiar elements in a new situation and to act in a manner that is appropriate to it. Good intuitive judgments come to mind with the same immediacy as "Doggie!"

Kahneman avers that expert intuition, like the pre-K teacher who knows just what to do to calm an angry child about to throw a block, is actually not intuition at all. These experts are instantaneously drawing on many years of experience and a vast knowledge base, often without realizing they are doing so. The difference between the toddler's thinking and the expert's thinking is only in the amount and sophistication of the information they process. Nonetheless, a young child's developing language is just as "miraculous" as an expert's sharp judgment, despite being much more commonplace, because both entail rapid use of higher-order thinking to accomplish a very complex mental task.

This example illustrates that higher-order thinking is needed to learn to speak a language, but once established, most language use entails the LOT skill of simple and automatic recall. This is just one example in which very young children use HOT skills, while older children and adults use LOT skills for the same task. Learning to do something new that is complex requires much more deliberate attention and mental effort than doing that same thing once it is fully learned. Remember how it felt and what you were thinking when driving on a highway for the first time? Compare that to how it feels and what you think about now when driving on a highway.

New Thinking about Infants' Thinking

Preverbal infants are also capable of higher-order thinking, which until recently was assumed to be far beyond their ability. The compelling evidence for this comes from researchers at Yale University's Infant Cognition Center who conducted clever experiments in which preverbal infants, some as young as three months, demonstrated the ability to make moral judgments that favor positive social behavior. About 80 percent of the babies in the study showed a preference for the puppet that helped another puppet open the lid of a box over the puppet that closed the lid (Hamlin, Wynn, and Bloom 2007). Subsequent experiments determined that a large majority of eight-month-old babies could make simple inferences (Hamlin, Newman, and Wynn 2009) and that babies between ten and twelve months were biased favorably toward a puppet that was similar to them—it had the same food preference—and biased against a puppet that was not similar to them—it had a different food preference (Mahajan and Wynn 2012).

We have known for some time that from birth our brains are hardwired (have a built-in capacity and predilection) for developing language (Chomsky 1965) and for understanding the basis of math, called the approximate number system (Dehaene 2011; Feigenson, Dehaene, and Spelke 2004). However, it now appears that we are also hardwired for making moral judgments, drawing inferences, holding certain biases, and undoubtedly for much more that is yet to be determined. The babies in the Yale studies would not be able to demonstrate many LOT skills, such as recalling and following directions, but they could demonstrate a range of

HOT skills. It will be several years before we expect them to be able to name various colors, but these experiments show babies can distinguish between colors and imbue them with particular qualities: the "good" and "bad" puppets were identical except for the color of their shirts.

Avoiding Thinking Errors and Countering Deceptions with HOT Skills

HOT skills are needed to avoid being misled by our own thinking errors or being tricked by the faulty thinking behind deceptive statements we hear or read. Some of these statements are not intentionally deceptive, but many are, especially those from advertisers, salespeople, politicians, commentators, and others who want to influence our thinking. Countering faulty thinking is very challenging, but with a great deal of practice, even preschoolers can learn to recognize some of the more common thinking errors. With continuous practice, most third graders will be able to catch some of their own thinking errors and parse many types of misleading statements to determine the intent of the speaker or writer and avoid being misled or deceived.

Mental Shortcuts

Of the many types of thinking errors, mental shortcuts are among the most common and most problematic because they are so easy to make. Also called heuristics, they can be positive and useful because they reduce the amount of time and effort it takes to form opinions or make decisions. They are important aspects of math, technology, and ethics. They help emergency room staff make good decisions quickly. A shortcut, after all, is a good thing if it gets you where you need to go more efficiently. However, these types of mental shortcuts have been developed deliberately and purposefully, while most mental shortcuts are made intuitively (automatically or subconsciously), which is another way of saying there is very little thinking going on. A familiar example of this is jumping to a conclusion. Here, very little effort is made to think about possible reasons for what is happening. There is no generative higher-order thinking.

Another example of a mental shortcut involves making false associations. When asked to rate the qualities of the people in a set of photos, adults and children alike will rate attractive people as being nicer and more trustworthy than unattractive people, although males tend to do this more than females (Kahneman 2011; Hines 2010; Halpern 2013). Attractiveness, the ultimate superficial characteristic, is used as a mental shortcut substituting for the more time-consuming and challenging task of making an evaluation based on sufficient reliable information. Mental shortcuts use LOT and MOT skills where HOT skills are needed, in this case, identifying instead of parsing and categorizing instead of evaluating. A person who has parsing skills would respond to the task by saying, "I don't know. I can't determine a person's character from her appearance!"

Stereotyping is closely related to making false associations. Stereotyping entails assigning a characteristic to an entire group or class of people. Even when they are positive ("All Asian students are smart"), they are harmful because they are misleading and not true.

Yet another type of mental shortcut is believing that the reason something happens or exists can be found in the inherent quality of a thing or person, rather than for external or more complex reasons. It is a mental shortcut that seeks information from the most obvious and readily available source. This is also called the inherence heuristic (Cimpian and Salomon 2014). A child may believe that wind is created by the swaying of tree branches and leaves. An adult may believe that people are good at math or playing the piano only because they were born with an inherent ability or talent. In the *SnapsHOT* Orange Is the New Green, on pages 146–148, the child views speed—how fast a bicycle can go—as an inherent quality of the bicycle, rather than as a combination of the will and ability of the rider and the mechanics of the bicycle. As students gain HOT skills and practice analyzing, they develop the awareness and ability to avoid relying on these mental shortcuts.

Thinking Biases

Stereotyping, described earlier, is also a type of thinking bias. Thinking biases are errors made by favoring one perspective over other perspectives without thinking through which perspectives are the most accurate. The stereotype about Asian students being smart ignores other possible perspectives: they work hard, care about doing well in school, like to learn, want to make themselves and their families proud, are ambitious, or work collaboratively with other students. While there are many other types of thinking biases, two of the most common are *optimism bias* and *confirmation bias*.

Optimism bias leads people to believe that things are better than they actually are or that things will turn out well regardless of what they do or don't do to affect the outcome. "Everything will be fine" and "Hope for the best" are two common expressions that reflect optimism bias. While having a positive attitude is a good thing, optimism bias often leads people to avoid dealing with problems, to not take the time and effort to think critically, and to make assessments that result in poor decisions. Common types of optimism biases among young students include having expectations that are too high or unrealistic—how many friends will come to their birthday parties, what presents they will receive, and how much fun it will be—and believing they know more than they do or are more skilled than they actually are. Inevitably, optimism bias leads to disappointment.

Confirmation bias is what leads people to believe fake news. We are attuned to hearing and believing information that confirms the views we already hold. Information that provides other perspectives or contradicts what we believe is conveniently ignored or dismissed. Many people will even believe a ridiculous claim or story if it aligns with what they believe. This makes confirmation bias particularly pernicious. Teachers can help students become aware of their confirmation biases through fun activities and interactions. They can respond to statements from students such as "I don't like science—it's boring. I'm not going to be a scientist," with "Yes, I know. A boring research study found that students who don't like science also don't play video games because there is too much boring science used in creating them!"

Thinking Deceptions

Students also need HOT skills to avoid being deceived by misleading statements they hear or read. Although the examples of such statements listed below sound sophisticated, it is not difficult to make them concrete and understandable to young learners. There are many activities throughout the book that do this, including the *Cognitivity* Brain Baits, which follows this section.

- Hyperbole: Greatly exaggerating, including making statements that begin "You never . . ." or "You always . . . ," or claiming that an idea or belief is ridiculous or impossible without offering a reason or proof. A more child-friendly phrase for this is "You exaggerate." Usually the intention of hyperbole is to end a discussion.

- Fallacy of composition: Claiming that what is true of a part must be true of the whole. A more child-friendly phrase for this is "It's just a piece of the puzzle, not the whole thing."

- Red herring: A statement that distracts from the topic or changes the topic to one more acceptable to the speaker (changing the subject). There are many red herring strategies, such as answering a different question from the one asked and attacking the speaker's credibility rather than the speaker's ideas. A more child-friendly phrase for this is "creating a distraction" or "avoiding the question."

- False dichotomy: Believing or claiming that there are only two possible answers or solutions (yes or no, all or none, right or wrong) when there are more. A child-friendly term is "either-or thinking."

- Leading the witness: Statements or questions that attempt to get a particular response, such as "Don't you agree?" "It's perfectly obvious that . . . ," or "Everyone knows that . . ." A more child-friendly phrase is "You should think the way I think."

- Shifting the burden of proof: Making a claim without evidence and requiring the other person to refute it. A more child-friendly phrase for this is "Prove me wrong."

There are, of course, many other types of deceptive statements. The ability to parse these fallacies depends on the ability to recognize them. With teacher-guided practice, even very young learners can begin to develop these abilities. Brain baits is one teaching technique for doing this in an enjoyable way.

COGNITIVITY: BRAIN BAITS

"This is the story of Goldilocks and the Three Gorillas." Brain baits, such as this one, create cognitive dissonance in a playful way. Our minds have a strong and immediate need to resolve the dissonance, thus triggering MOT skills such as A/D thinking. Cognitive dissonance can be created by telling a blatantly false or intentionally misleading comment, which teachers can easily and quickly slip into lessons or discussions, as in the Goldilocks example above. But brain baits can also be connected to content learning and be more subtle and complex as students gain skills and become more sophisticated thinkers. Because they require students to catch and correct errors, brain baits help them learn to parse deceptive statements.

There is an example of a teacher using brain baits with the story of Henny Penny in the *SnapsHOT Is the Sky Falling?* on page 105. The story is essentially about problems caused by the thinking error of jumping to conclusions, especially in believing an outlandish statement because the messenger instills fear and creates stress. Henny Penny doesn't do this intentionally; she really believes the sky is falling. But appealing to fear and using scare tactics are common deceptions used intentionally by advertisers, politicians, and others. The teacher reinforces the lessons of the story and helps the children practice parsing with brain baits. When a paper falls from the wall, she shouts, "The ceiling is falling!" She then helps them identify the thinking error and refute it with incisive questions, visual evidence, and deductive thinking.

The brain baits in the *SnapsHOT* below occur during a discussion related to the concepts of wild and tame (see the description of the theme Wild and Tame, on pages 119–120).

SNAPSHOT: "CHEETAHED"?

Teacher: Here is a picture of my cheetah.

Students: That's a dog!

Teacher: No, no, no. You can't trick me; I know it's a cheetah. (shift the burden of proof)

Students: IT'S A DOG!!

Teacher: That's ridiculous. How can you possibly think it's a dog? (dismiss with hyperbole)

Student A: Cheetahs have spots!

Teacher: I know that! Look here on its back. There are spots. (fallacy of composition)

Student B: They have spots all over.

Teacher: Lots of things have spots all over. Like Dalmatians. Didn't you see that movie? And something else that has spots is . . . (red herring)

Student C: They don't have floppy ears.

Student D: They're wild. They're not pets!

Teacher: That sounds like faulty thinking to me. A pet can be a wild animal or something that once was a wild animal. People have pet snakes. (models parsing a false dichotomy and throws another red herring) But my pet isn't a wild animal . . . so, she's really not a cheetah?

Students: NOOO!

Teacher: Well, they told me at the pet store it was a cheetah! But I think they "cheetahed" me. Do you think I can return it?

(In response, some students laugh, some look incredulous, some look skeptical, some look confused, and some look concerned about their teacher's sanity.)

Teacher: Actually, I've grown to love my chee—my dog, so I guess I'll keep her. It doesn't really matter how her ears look or if she's a dog or a cheetah. She's a great companion with a sweet personality. *That* is what's important. (models parsing)

In this next *SnapsHOT*, a second-grade teacher discusses the life of Abraham Lincoln after students have read two short biographies in the days just prior to Presidents' Day.

SNAPSHOT: LINCOLN THINKIN'

Teacher: What to you is the most important thing about Abraham Lincoln or the most important thing that he did? (asks students to parse)

(Several students contribute ideas: he was poor but grew up to be a president; he freed the slaves; he won the Civil War.)

Teacher: I agree with all of you. I really admire what a great orator he was, too. He could really give a speech! And everyone loved him and his ideas. Our country wasn't divided like it is now; every person in America loved him, isn't that right? (leading the witness)

(There are a few nods but no responses. Silence for about fifteen seconds.)

Teacher: You let me trick you. I told you something that isn't true, but my question at the end fooled you. It stopped you from deep thinking, from parsing what I said. Or maybe it stopped you from telling me I was wrong. What was my question and how did it trick you?

During the discussion that follows, the teacher reminds the students that nothing they read about Lincoln said that everyone loved him, and much of what they read were descriptions of the deep divisions between the North and South. A supporter of the Confederacy hated Lincoln so much that he assassinated him.

Then the teacher helps the students understand deceptive thinking in the statement.

Teacher: Even if he was widely loved, it couldn't be possible that *everyone* loved him. That is a *gigantic* exaggeration. And I just said another one! (hyperbole)

Now I'm going to say ten things about Lincoln. For each statement, write down the number 1 if you think it is true, 2 if you think it is false, 3 if you think it *could* be or is *probably* true, but we don't know for sure, and 4 if you think it is an opinion. Don't let me fool you with misleading questions, exaggerations, or other tricks. Remember, if any part of my statement is not true, then the whole statement is not true. I might try to distract you from realizing that I said something false by saying some true things in the same statement.

1. Lincoln was the sixteenth president.

2. Lincoln was the best president.

3. Lincoln never used a computer to write his speeches; he wrote them with a pen and paper.

4. Lincoln didn't like using a computer to write his speeches; he preferred to write them with a pen and paper.

5. Lincoln believed in natural rights, like freedom, for everyone.

6. Lincoln was born in a log cabin.

7. Lincoln was born in Kentucky in 1809 and died there in 1865, just five days after the end of the Civil War.

8. Lincoln liked the theater; he liked to see plays.

9. Lincoln's signature on the Declaration of Independence was the first and the largest.

10. If it wasn't for Lincoln, the South would have won the Civil War.

The teacher facilitates a discussion about the statements and the types of deceptions they reflect. Then the students are given the challenge to write four different statements about Lincoln: one true, one false, one that could be true, and one that is an opinion. They do this working in small groups and test each other.

Conclusion

The critical thinking HOT skills of parsing and evaluating are the key skills for avoiding thinking errors and countering deceptive statements. Teachers of young students can start the process of developing these HOT skills, and they can do it with intention and skill, by applying the concepts and ideas in this book. Just as establishing good nutrition habits early sets the foundation for a healthier life, developing basic-level HOT skills early sets the foundation for a more productive and purposeful life. For most people, becoming proficient at speaking a foreign language or playing a musical instrument is much harder if they start lessons as an adult, or even as an adolescent, rather than as a child. The same is true for becoming proficient at using HOT skills.

At birth, the human brain is one-third the weight of the adult brain. This means that two-thirds of its mass is formed while in interaction with other people and the environment. And nearly all that mass is formed in the first six years of life. The active part of the brain consists of billions of brain cells (neurons) and trillions of connections between them (synapses) that are formed, trimmed, re-formed, weakened, and strengthened during those first six years. So when we help children master HOT skills early, the connections in their brains for critical thinking are being formed and strengthened. These neural connections will expand and last a lifetime if teachers and parents continue to provide opportunities for students to use them at increasingly advanced levels.

The ability of infants to prefer helpful behavior over mean behavior, as with other rudimentary HOT skills, appears to be inborn. If not nurtured, this and all other hardwired capabilities will remain at a rudimentary level, and some may even fade. But they will easily and naturally flourish with informed teaching and a good balance of challenge and support over time. The inborn abilities that are counterproductive in today's world, such as biases against people who are perceived to be different, can be replaced as children grow and gain more advanced thinking skills. Now, with new and more complete knowledge about thinking skills and strategies to promote them, we can be more intentional and capable in nurturing HOT skills from the time children are very young.

Key Ideas from This Chapter

- Children's thinking and adults' thinking are not substantively different. Even very young children are capable of every type of thinking, including most types of higher-order thinking. Adults and children make similar types of thinking errors and show preferences for certain categories of thinking over others. They do differ, however, in the level of complexity of their thinking, and adults have many more experiences and a greater knowledge base to draw from.

- Certain HOT skills appear to be inborn, as demonstrated by experiments with preverbal infants. The infants show preferences for puppets that are helpful over ones that are mean and puppets that are more like themselves over ones that are less so, and they show distain for puppets that are significantly different from them. Babies can also infer intent from behaviors and demonstrate several other HOT skills.

- Inborn HOT skills that are not nurtured and further developed will remain at a rudimentary level and can even fade away. Inborn HOT skills that are counterproductive can be replaced as children grow and develop more advanced thinking skills.

- HOT skills help students avoid thinking errors as well as avoid being deceived by misleading statements. The critical thinking skills of parsing and evaluating are particularly useful for this purpose.

Questions for Discussion

- Review the quote from Alison Gopnik at the beginning of the chapter, on page 88. How can teachers reconcile the need for students to have clear and explicit information with the need to learn to be innovative and generate original ideas?

- Discuss the role of schools and teachers in helping students use their HOT skills for positive purposes. What are some teaching and curricula strategies that can promote this?

- What are some examples of how the thinking of adults and children are similar and dissimilar?

- After reviewing examples of fake news stories that have been believed by many people, discuss the deceptive thinking strategies used by the writers and the types of thinking errors made by the readers who believed them.

- What are some other types of thinking errors that students have made that were not discussed in this chapter?

- What are some thinking deceptions that are targeted at young children?

Part 2
Learning to Think, Thinking to Learn

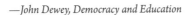

Give the pupils something to do, not something to learn; and the doing
is of such a nature as to demand thinking . . . learning naturally results.

—*John Dewey, Democracy and Education*

Guiding Principles for HOT Teaching and Learning:
Rigor and Joy

Part 1 of this book provided detailed information about the mental tools in the toolbox inside our heads. Now, with a good supply of high-quality mental tools and the knowledge of their functions and purposes, it's time to help students learn to use these tools. The most effective way we learn to use actual tools is in the process of accomplishing a real task, such as hanging a painting, fixing a leak, or making a potting bench. The same is true for learning to use HOT skills. The strategies and activities in this section engage students' higher-order thinking. And in the process of using HOT skills, they learn what they are, how they work, and how to use them effectively and at increasingly advanced levels.

There are important guiding principles for learning to use any powerful or complex hardware tool: follow safety precautions, carefully read the operating instructions, ensure that it is the right tool for the job, check that it is in good working order before using it, know how to prepare the work space and materials, and, finally, know how to maintain it in good condition. This chapter describes four guiding principles for facilitating the development of students' HOT skills and provides example scenarios, or *SnapsHOTs*, to illustrate how they are applied in practice.

The four guiding principles are as follows:

1. HOT skills are taught implicitly *and* explicitly.
2. Activities that promote HOT skills are flexible and responsive.
3. Activities are challenging *and* enjoyable.
4. Activities help students gain insight, understanding, and an appreciation for the subject, in addition to skills and knowledge.

These guiding principles help teachers effectively promote the development of HOT skills and reach all students. A full review of theories of differences among students in their learning styles and needs, types of intelligences, cultural influences, preferences, and other factors is beyond the scope of this book; however, the individualized student-centered practices reflected in these guiding principles are responsive to all learners regardless of cultural and individual differences.

HOT Skills Are Taught Implicitly *and* Explicitly

There are curricula developed to teach thinking skills specifically and exclusively. Some, like the Instrumental Enrichment program (Feuerstein, Feuerstein, and Falik 2010), use abstract problems, such as finding patterns in meaningless figures. Some, like the Productive Thinking curriculum (Covington, et al. 1972), use mystery stories. And some, like the Cognitive Research Trust program (de Bono 1985), use group discussions of common problems. Each program uses a similar format for its sessions. Students are given examples of a higher-order thinking skill and an explanation of the skill and then practice applying it in different, usually hypothetical, situations (Willingham 2007).

The results from a large body of research on how best to teach thinking skills indicate that explicitly teaching thinking skills (but not necessarily through an established curriculum) is important and necessary (Collins 2014). A number of experts in the field make a compelling case that explicit instruction of thinking skills is best done in the context of content-matter lessons and when teachable moments offer opportunities (Abrami et al. 2015; Goodwin 2017). Robert Swartz, who directs the Center for Teaching Thinking (www.teach-think.org), calls this "infusion" (Swartz et al. 2010). This approach is reflected in most of the examples of activities—*SnapsHOTs, Cognitivities,* and *ThinkinGames*—throughout this book. Implicit methods of teaching HOT skills are also important, and they complement and support explicit methods. The primary method of implicit instruction in this book involves teachers modeling HOT skills. However, for implicit teaching to have an impact on students' thinking, HOT skills must be modeled often and skillfully. There are a few strategies and techniques presented in chapters 8 and 9 that are designed to teach HOT skills explicitly and are not infused into content learning. But these are done through games and other enjoyable activities. Here is a *SnapsHOT* of "infusion" in action. HOT skills are taught explicitly in the context of a well-known story.

SNAPSHOT: IS THE SKY FALLING?

After reading the story of Henny Penny (a.k.a. Chicken Little) to older preschoolers, Ms. Silvia asks them questions about why Henny Penny thinks that the sky is falling when she is hit on the head by an acorn. A discussion follows about how being afraid and feeling panicky affects our ability to use higher-order thinking or even lower-order thinking, and can cause us to make thinking errors. New vocabulary and concepts are introduced, such as "jumping to a conclusion" and "cause and effect." The students are asked for other examples of jumping to a conclusion, and Ms. Silvia provides one or two as well.

Later in the day, Ms. Silvia leads small groups of students to act out several alternative versions of the story. In one version, the other animals help Henny Penny calm down and ask her to explain how she knows the sky is falling and to think about other possible causes of something hitting her head.

Over the course of the week, Ms. Silvia takes advantage of some teachable moments, much to the children's delight. When a drawing falls from the wall during circle time, Ms. Silvia shouts, "The ceiling is falling! The ceiling is falling!" She encourages her students to try to convince her that the ceiling is not falling. At another time, when the class is outside on a warm day in late spring, a child slips and nearly falls. Ms. Silvia says, "Oops, I'm glad you didn't fall. Be careful of the patches of ice!" The children try to refute her logic when she says, "Ice is slippery, Gino slipped, so there must be ice on the ground." This logical thinking error involving causes and effects is also called a *syllogism*: while the first two statements are true, the third concluding statement is false. They finally investigate and notice a small spot of oil (parsing). Ms. Silvia helps them figure out that if they put a little sand over the spot, it will be less slippery.

Several days later, Ms. Silvia reads the story again but focuses on the issue of the other animals not parsing Henny Penny's bad information, from which the fox correctly infers (another critical thinking skill) that all of the animals can be easily fooled.

Activities That Promote HOT Skills Are Responsive to All Learners

While there are many theories about the various ways people tend to think and learn, the concept of field-dependent versus field-independent cognitive styles (Witkin et al. 1962) has been widely accepted for decades. Field-dependent, or contextual, thinkers perceive that the identity of everyone and the meaning and purpose of everything are primarily provided by their contexts, relationships, and connections. This type of thinking is sometimes referred to as collectivistic. Field-independent, or discrete, thinkers view all people and things as primarily having an individual, unique identity independent of any contextual factors, connections, or relationships. This type of thinking is sometimes referred to as individualistic. Most contextual thinkers have stronger practical thinking skills than conceptual thinking skills, while the opposite is true of most discrete thinkers. Contextual thinkers tend to "see the forest but not the trees." Discrete thinkers tend to "see the trees but not the forest."

There is a link between contextual or discrete thinking and national cultures. The values, beliefs, and practices of some national cultures, such as North Korea's, strongly promote contextual thinking, while in other countries, such as the United States, they strongly promote discrete thinking. All national cultures can be characterized by the degree to which they promote one thinking style more than the other. This characteristic is thoroughly embedded within all aspects of society and has deep and ancient roots in the founding of every country (Hofstede 2011). As a result, for most people, their thinking style is very solid and stable and resistant to change.

Many students from immigrant families come from countries whose national cultures embrace contextual thinking more than discrete thinking. Students who are contextual thinkers will likely face some challenges learning to use HOT skills and applying them regularly. To make it easier for them, teachers can ensure that tasks and activities requiring critical or creative thinking skills have a meaningful context, a use and purpose, and a strong social component. The following *SnapsHOT* illustrates how this can be done.

SNAPSHOT: A SPECIAL LUNCH

The school kitchen staff has offered to make a special lunch every Friday. Each class is given the opportunity to choose the menu for one of these special lunch days. The students in each class will have to come to an agreement about the style of cooking, the main dish, a side dish, and the dessert they will request. Ms. Nguyen uses this opportunity to engage her first graders in a data-collecting, graphing, and decision-making activity. She starts with a whole class discussion and brainstorming activity, which she records on a whiteboard in four columns: Style, Main Course, Side Dish, and Dessert. First, the students identify three styles of cooking that they like: American, Mexican, and Vietnamese. These are the three national cultures of the students in the class. For each style, they name two main courses and one side dish. They name two desserts, ice cream and brownies, which are unrelated to a cooking style, as that proved difficult and unpopular. Ms. Nguyen then reminds her students that they will need to choose *as a class* only one style, and one main course, side dish, and dessert.

She leads them in a lesson on sets and determining the possible number of sets they can choose from, each set being a lunch comprising three items and one style. Each lunch set is assigned a number and name. The students have fun working in pairs to make up names, such as "Yummy Noodles," "Picnic Power," and "*3 Bs*—Burritos, Beans, Brownies."

Later in the day, Ms. Nguyen leads them in making a bar graph of their choices. The graph has twelve numbers on the x-axis, one for each possible lunch set. Using a secret ballot process, each student writes down the number and name of the lunch set that they like the best on a blue sticky note and their second choice on a yellow sticky note. Starting with their first choices, the students put their sticky notes in their appropriate spots to create a vertical bar graph. After Ms. Nguyen helps them "read" the results, they post their second choices and review the results again. "Reading the results" consists of determining which lunch sets have the most votes, fewest votes, the same number of votes, zero votes, and so on. Then Ms. Nguyen asks a question: "Set five got zero votes; does that mean that everyone in the class does not like the food in that lunch?" She guides a short discussion to help them understand that because the items in that lunch are also on other lunch sets that were selected as favorites, it cannot mean that no one likes it. "Also," she states, "you may like something just fine but then choose something else that you like even more."

Ms. Nguyen leads a discussion about different ways they can make a choice, other than just selecting the one with the most votes, including choosing by consensus after a discussion or, she jokes, letting the teacher decide. In the end, the students agree to select the one with the most votes.

Two of the lunch sets clearly have more votes than the others, but the one that has the most total votes has more second choice votes and fewer first choice votes. She asks the students, "Would it be more fair to choose the one with the most first choice votes or the most total votes, or is there a way to count both?" After a lively discussion among the students, Ms. Nguyen describes how to count both sets of votes fairly by making first choice votes worth more than second choice votes, resulting in a total that shows which one has the most overall value. (She avoids the technical term for this, *weighting*, as it would likely confuse first graders.)

To illustrate the concept, she makes two stacks of coins. One stack has ten coins: seven nickels and three dimes. The other has only eight coins: two nickels and six dimes. Together, they add up the amount of money in each stack and find that the smaller stack is worth more. Ms. Nguyen suggests that second choice votes count as half a vote so that two second choice votes are equal to one first choice vote, just as two nickels are equal to one dime and a nickel is worth half as much as a dime. Upon counting the votes this way, the lunch set with fewer total votes but more first choice votes has greater value. Some of the practical thinkers among the students still have difficulty accepting that the lunch set with the tallest bar was not selected. Ms. Nguyen reminds them, "Appearances can be misleading, so look beyond the surface and think deep. Because something is bigger, it does not mean it's more valuable. Nickels are bigger than dimes." She then has the students congratulate each other on their hard work and higher-order thinking abilities.

Ms. Nguyen elicits the strengths of her contextual thinking students when they express personal preferences for food and see their cultures' cuisine represented and appreciated. The entire process involves a decision that requires sensitivity to the feelings and preferences of all the members of the peer group. They work in pairs to create a name for a lunch set, which also provides an opportunity for creative thinkers to shine. They are actively involved when they put their sticky notes on the graph. Ms. Nguyen knows that fairness is a concept they readily understand and care about, thereby putting them on a more equal footing with the discrete thinkers during the discussion. Having students congratulate each other is a small but significant gesture to support the values of mutual respect and group harmony in the classroom.

In addition, she embeds a few challenges for her more advanced contextual thinkers in the activity. The challenges are aimed at helping these students gain skills and feel comfortable thinking discretely and conceptually, as future schoolwork will increasingly demand such thinking. The challenges include making an individual decision about their preferred lunch set and understanding that their teacher was not serious about allowing herself to make the decision. The final challenge was understanding that the tallest bar on the graph is not the one with the greatest value.

Among the many HOT skills that Ms. Nguyen promoted was representing a number and name for each lunch set (logical thinking skill), generating ideas for naming lunch sets (creative thinking skill), and calculating the number of lunch sets (logical thinking skill). She engaged students in a simple analysis (thinking process) by inferring information from the graph (critical thinking skill) and deducing information to respond to her question about the lunch set with zero votes (logical thinking skill). They used A/D thinking to explore several different ways that the group can collectively decide on a lunch set (logical thinking skill) and to infer that Ms. Nguyen was not serious when she suggested that she make the decision (critical thinking skill). Another analysis took place when they discussed the issue of fairness in determining which lunch set has the most value. Critical thinking in general was defined explicitly when Ms. Nguyen told them to look beyond appearances and think deeply.

Activities Are Challenging *and* Enjoyable

Dr. Lilian Katz, one of our leading sages in early childhood education, makes a strong argument for teaching practices that focus more on intellectual goals for young learners and active project-based learning and less on academic goals and formal instruction. She defines intellectual goals as "those that address the life of the mind in its fullest sense (e.g., reasoning, predicting, analyzing, questioning)" (Katz 2015, 1). Essentially, she is calling for more activities that prompt higher-order thinking. But Dr. Katz is not only concerned about formal instruction; she is concerned about unchallenging, intellectually weak practices that are all too common in early childhood classrooms: "While intellectual dispositions may be weakened or even damaged by excessive and premature formal instruction, they are also not likely to be strengthened by many of the mindless, trivial if not banal activities frequently offered in child care, preschool, and kindergarten programs" (2).

What makes an activity challenging and intellectually rigorous? In short, it engages students' HOT skills and is targeted near the top of children's current ability levels. For second graders, asking them to complete twenty-five subtraction problems on a work sheet will be arduous because it requires much time and effort. But it will also be tedious as it involves mostly LOT skills and repetition. Quantity is no substitute for quality in teaching and learning. A quality, challenging assignment, for example, would ask second graders to create and then solve four subtraction problems related to the scores, points, or standings of teams in a sports league of their choosing. It is challenging because it requires the use of HOT skills. For most students, it will not feel tedious, and for many students it will be enjoyable.

When arithmetic is taught only through LOT skills, most of the advanced or quick-to-learn students are bored, and most of the struggling students do not learn it. Except for the most jaded, nearly all students want to engage with an intellectually rigorous curriculum, and they will rise to the challenges it offers. Also, when the curriculum is rigorous, there are fewer problematic behaviors because students are involved in learning and are not bored or "lost."

What does this look like in action? To answer this question, let's revisit the activity described in chapter 6 in which the teacher asked her students to name vegetables (page 88). The content areas of the lesson were language and cultural knowledge, and the specific content was to know the names of vegetables. The methodology the teacher used was to ask the whole group questions to elicit the one correct answer. The goals of the lesson were to improve students' language skills (vocabulary), knowledge of a variety of vegetables, and, perhaps, cultural knowledge of autumn—the theme for the month. How could this curriculum activity be modified to be more challenging and enjoyable? How can the same content be taught through activities that promote HOT skills?

The Activity Could Be More Learner Centered

The students had few opportunities to ask questions, discuss the qualities of the vegetables, or make connections to prior knowledge or to their daily lives. Discussing questions from students is an essential strategy for building HOT skills. The activity asked students to use LOT skills—imitate, memorize, and recall—as the way to increase students' knowledge of vegetables. The students were not allowed to touch, smell, or taste them (although a few students did this later during a small-group cooking activity), which would have provided more complete knowledge of each vegetable. There was one question throughout the activity: "What is the name of this vegetable?" As previously suggested, the teacher could ask how two very different-looking vegetables could both be peppers. Here are some other questions that would lead to interesting discussions and the use of a variety of HOT skills:

- What makes a vegetable a vegetable?
- What about this vegetable tells you that it is a pumpkin?
- What are all the different foods that are made from potatoes that you have eaten?
- Which vegetables do we need to cook to eat and why?
- Which vegetables do we usually eat raw, and which ones can we eat both ways, raw and cooked?

The Activity Could Have a Context and Be Made More Enjoyable through Play

Providing a context benefits more than just the contextual thinkers. At any age, most people learn better and retain information longer if there is a purpose or context for the activity, a reason for taking the time and making the effort to learn something new. It's the difference between learning to speak French sitting in a classroom in Montpelier, Vermont, or while living with a French family in Montpellier, France. Almost always, learning is more enjoyable when there is a meaningful context. For this activity, one effective way to provide a context is to create an imaginary situation such as a farm, a farmers' market, or a grocery store. The students then learn, or practice recalling, the names of the vegetables in the course of buying and selling them.

The Activity Could Be Restructured to Be More Thorough

A common problem with many curricula activities and curricula in general is that they cover too much information too quickly. They are more like a swamp than a lake—wide and shallow rather than confined and deep. Covering less information more thoroughly is more meaningful and satisfying—much like how it feels to swim in a lake as compared to wade through a swamp—and provides many more opportunities to promote HOT skills. The activity could be made more thorough by showing fewer vegetables and exploring each one in more detail. It would free up time to feel, smell, and taste them and for the teacher to ask questions and lead discussions that promote HOT skills, as previously described.

Activities Help Students Gain Insights, Understanding, and Appreciation

This principle is potentially the most impactful of the four. To plan activities that lead to insights, understanding, and appreciation of the subject, teachers need to know many strategies that elicit students' use of HOT skills. HOT skills are the tools that unlock insights, facilitate understanding, and build appreciation. These goals may seem formal and challenging to achieve, but they can be met through common activities, as in the following *SnapsHOT*.

SNAPSHOT: HARRIET 'ROUND THE MOUNTAIN

Jamaal, a kindergarten teacher, is also a talented musician. Among the many songs he has taught his students, "She'll Be Coming 'Round the Mountain" is a favorite. It has the fun challenge of repeating all the sounds and actions in reverse order ("choo-choo," "whoa back," "hi babe,"), and Jamaal and the children enjoy making up silly verses.

When developing lesson plans, Jamaal regularly searches the internet for information and ideas on ways to promote insight, understanding, and appreciation for his activities. One day, Jamaal finds a version of the song with a verse he had never heard before: "We'll all sing hallelujah when she comes." This seems odd to him, so he reads a bit more about the song.

The next day, he shares what he learned with his class. He tells them, "Before singing 'She'll Be Coming 'Round the Mountain' today, I want to read a book to you that will teach us something about the song. It's called *An Apple for Harriet Tubman* (Turner 2016)." After reading and facilitating a short discussion about the book, Jamaal states, "So, you probably want to know what a book about slavery and the Underground Railroad can teach us about our song 'She'll Be Coming 'Round the Mountain.' Well, it is a very old song, and we don't know who made up the tune or wrote the words. But we do know that a long time ago it had different words. It was a religious song that people sang in church. Then the words and the name of the song were changed by slaves to make it a song that celebrates the Underground Railroad. Why do you think they didn't use the words *slave* or *Underground Railroad* in the song? Which words or phrases in the song could be about the Underground Railroad? We'll need to do some higher-order thinking to find out."

After a brief discussion in which Jamaal gives other examples of hidden messages in songs and stories, he tells them, "Now let's sing the song and think about slavery, Harriet Tubman, and the Underground Railroad. After, we'll talk about how we felt singing the song this time compared to how we felt singing it before."

Among the important insights and understandings that Jamaal gave his kindergartners were the following:

- Things change and transform over time.

- Even the most powerless people can find ways to give themselves some power when they use creative thinking.

- Things are not always what they appear to be on the surface.

- Subject areas are not usually distinct and are often integrated (music, literacy, and history in this example).

- A single thing, such as a song, can have more than one purpose or meaning simultaneously or sequentially.

- There are many interesting things to learn from history.

Conclusion

Perhaps the most important aspect of the lesson described in the above *SnapsHOT* was Jamaal's modeling of the value of intellectual pursuits. He taught students by example that obtaining more information and gaining a fuller understanding of an event, person, work of art, scientific concept, or song can deepen our feelings about it and strengthen our appreciation. While this guiding principle is critically important for promoting HOT skills, when teachers apply all four principles they can be most effective. Teaching HOT skills implicitly and explicitly, implementing activities that are responsive to all types of learners from all cultures, and building on students' strengths ensures that teaching and learning activities will be sufficiently individualized. And finally, when these activities are in equal measure challenging and enjoyable, students will be fully engaged and developing the intellectual capacities to be successful in school and in life.

Key Ideas from This Chapter

There are four guiding principles for effectively promoting the development of students' HOT skills:

- HOT skills are taught implicitly *and* explicitly.

- Activities that promote HOT skills are responsive to all learners.

- Activities are challenging *and* enjoyable.

- Activities help students gain insight, understanding, and an appreciation for the subject, in addition to skills and knowledge.

Collectively, these four guiding principles promote HOT teaching by ensuring that all students will be engaged in learning and in the process of honing their HOT skills and developing new ones.

Questions for Discussion

- Discuss examples of using other guiding principles for different teaching endeavors. How can your experiences inform the use of these guiding principles for HOT teaching?

- Teaching literacy explicitly and implicitly but contextually happens easily because print is so visible and ubiquitous and so much of teaching and learning involves reading and writing. Thinking is much less visible, however. Discuss various ways that thinking could be made more visible.

- Discuss the thinking strengths of particular students (current and past). Identify as many different types of thinking strengths as possible.

- Identify an example in your life when gaining more information about a situation, artwork, issue, or person's circumstances led to a change in your views. 🧠

HOT Strategies for HOT Teaching:
Serious Fun

When using powerful and complex hardware tools, there are general strategies or practices for applying the guiding principles. For example, regarding the guiding principle "Check that the tool is in good working order before using it," a good practice for cutting tools is to check if the blade needs to be sharpened or replaced. In the same way, there are general strategies for applying the guiding principles to engage young students' higher-order thinking. This chapter offers strategies for all four principles but emphasizes those that make challenging activities enjoyable and enjoyable activities challenging. There are games, play, and playful materials that facilitate intellectually rigorous thinking, and there are intellectually rigorous math and literacy activities that are playful. The HOT strategies in this chapter maximize opportunities for teachers to develop students' HOT skills.

Cooperative, Collaborative, and Social Learning

Learning with partners or in small groups should be the default mode, the rule rather than the exception. By requiring students to articulate and accurately communicate what they are thinking, social learning adds complexity to thinking tasks and fosters the development of more advanced levels of thinking. In addition, students need to be able to understand what others are communicating and their implications, which may involve inferring, interpreting, changing perspectives, reframing, and other HOT skills. Of course, this can't be left to chance. Teachers use these interactions as opportunities to gently correct faulty thinking and misunderstandings, to help students use a HOT skill at a more advanced level, or to give them practice using a new or more effective HOT skill for the task. Social learning also presents opportunities to improve students' social skills and ability to work in groups while practicing higher-order thinking. Negotiating roles and tasks, for example, usually involves the thinking processes of making decisions and solving problems, to a greater or lesser degree.

The *ThinkinGame* below involves students working in pairs or small groups. It is a bit challenging, so it may require practice over time.

THINKINGAME: RHYME TIME

With a partner or in small groups, students make drawings or plan physical demonstrations that depict two rhyming words, which their classmates must guess. For example, they may draw a fat cat or a red bed. (Creating the drawings requires imagining, generating ideas, planning, and representing; guessing the rhyming words requires inferring, deducing, and transferring.) The rhyming words can also be part of a short phrase, such as "pup in a cup" or "a mouse on a house." The mouse and house can be drawn on separate pieces of paper, and the students can show the mouse going on the house. In another version of the game, students use physical demonstrations rather than drawings. For example, one student hops, and the other students in the group look at her and laugh (a funny bunny). Props can also be used in demonstrations. A student might use a broom while his eyes are closed and head hangs down (sweeping while sleeping).

The game can be noncompetitive as described above or can be made competitive in a number of ways. Points can be awarded to the group or pair that guesses the rhyme correctly before the others. Points can also be awarded for the funniest or most clever rhyme using a voting process like the one described in the *Cognitivity* May the Best Map Win on page 77.

For preschoolers, the rhyming pictures can be made by the teacher for the children to guess. As they catch on to the game, the pictures can become more challenging. For older students who have become adept at playing Rhyme Time, the game can be extended to require more advanced levels of thinking by creating three-word rhymes and/or restricting the rhymes to a category, such as clothing (a blue shoe) or books and stories (the three bears go upstairs) or both (Goldilocks's socks). Rhyme Time employs the HOT strategy of *ThinkinGames* and addresses the content areas of art, drama, social skills, language and literature, and potentially more.

HOT Themes

A theme-based curriculum approach is more common in pre-K programs, but it is equally effective for kindergarten through third-grade classrooms. Actually, theme-based learning can be effective and powerful at every grade level, including postsecondary. My college freshman English literature professor assigned readings that were all related to the theme of justice. This compelling theme is the reason that I can still remember this class from 1969! We read the book of Job from the Bible, *Measure for Measure* by Shakespeare, and *One Flew Over the Cuckoo's Nest* by Ken Kesey, among other great works.

In theme-based curricula, the teaching of concepts, content area knowledge, and skills are integrated within activities that are linked by the theme. A theme creates a context, which makes learning easier for the many students who are contextual thinkers. Compared to teaching content knowledge discretely, this approach is more effective for developing HOT skills because it provides a clear purpose for thinking and learning. It is more attuned to the way children naturally learn (Buchsbaum et al. 2011; Gopnik 2016a) and more like the way thinking skills are applied in real-life situations. Also, students are more motivated to learn, particularly if the theme topic is compelling to them. Themes naturally lend themselves to project-based learning, which is the next strategy discussed in this chapter.

The selection of a theme is a bit of an art. An effective theme lends itself to activities that are intellectually rigorous, enjoyable, active and interactive, meaningful to students, and that engage higher-order thinking. HOT themes are effective themes that deal with significant issues in children's lives, issues that all children grapple with almost every day. Following is a sample of possible HOT themes:

- **No Fair!** explores the issue of fairness and involves learning, inventing, and practicing different techniques to make sure that the pizza is divided equally, that everyone gets a turn on the swing, and other potential injustices. It also involves understanding when and why equal treatment is not always what is most fair and how to know when the deck is stacked. For third graders, the theme can extend to social issues such as equity, equality, and justice.

- **Winning and Losing** addresses the issue of competition in its many forms and ways to depersonalize losing and be gracious in winning. The role that chance, luck, effort, skill, and practice play in winning and losing are explored. MOT and HOT skills that can contribute to winning, such as calculating, planning/strategizing, shifting perspective, and imagining, are practiced in the context of games and contests.

- **Luck Doesn't Last** is closely related to Winning and Losing and can be included as part of that unit. In this theme, the issue of chance is explored in more depth. A number of activities involve distinguishing between luck and skill. Students invent games and intentionally manipulate aspects of games to alter how much luck versus skill is involved in winning.

- **Good, Better, Best** is also related to Winning and Losing. This theme addresses the issue of unequal innate abilities among people. Among the goals of this theme are to help students understand and accept that some people have more ability or talent in certain areas than other people, although everyone has strengths and weaknesses. Activities help students understand that effort can bridge the ability gap and innate abilities usually dissipate without effort. Teachers model and encourage students to be happy for their classmates' achievements and inspired by them, rather than feel envious. Students work in groups on multimedia projects about a living person of their choosing who excels in some way.

- **Brain Power** addresses children's (mostly boys') struggles with "good and evil" and power and control as it relates to physical prowess and violence. Many children have misconceptions about physical power, which they learn from animated television shows and other media aimed at children, especially boys. They internalize the false notion that "good guys" are always more powerful than "bad guys." This leads a child to believe he can beat up or destroy anything or anybody that's "bad," no matter how big or strong, because he sees himself as the "good guy." This misconception logically leads to another misconception: violence is an acceptable solution to any conflict or threat because good will always defeat evil. A goal of the theme is for children to internalize the idea that brain power is mightier than physical power and the only way that a smaller and weaker animal or person can defeat or thwart a bigger and stronger animal or person is with brain power. Along with a variety of media literacy activities, there is an extended and deep investigation of brain power in many forms through reading and analyzing stories, fictional and real, in which people or characters use cleverness, cunning, quick thinking, preparation, foresight, strategy, and similar processes rather than force to solve conflicts or save themselves from danger. Stories with protagonists who are children or small characters are highlighted. Among these stories are the classic fairy tales "Puss in Boots" and "Tom Thumb," and many of Roald Dahl's books.

- **Me and We** deals with the tension between the individual and the collective, or self-identity and group identity. Activities help students learn the many ways to be a good group member while still being a strong, unique individual and to think and act independently while respecting the needs and rights of others. Among many other activities, the books of Leo Lionni, which address this issue—*Swimmy* ([1963] 2011), *Frederick* (1967), and *A Color of His Own* ([1975] 2006)—are read and discussed.

The most impactful HOT theme ideas come from carefully observing children and listening to their conversations over time. Often an issue that is concerning them emerges, as in the following *SnapsHOT*.

SNAPSHOT: WILD AND TAME

A photo book about African animals is a favorite of the younger children in Drew's after-school program, particularly the photos of lions, cheetahs, and other big cats. The book is a large coffee-table type of book with sharp, colorful photos, some of which depict grisly scenes of big cats capturing and tearing apart impalas and other prey. The children find these photos to be both scary and irresistible. Small groups of children look at the book together and have lively conservations, which include a good deal of squealing and oohing in addition to heated discussions about how to avoid being eaten by a lion.

In their play, children try to capture and "tame" other children who are pretending to be wild animals. Often, the "wild animals" let themselves be caught and tamed, but, after a short period, they revert back to being wild. They repeat this cycle many times with slight variations and often switch roles. Drew believes that this provides a healthy way for the children to act "bad" without consequences, to grapple with issues of impulse control, and to learn to manage their anger and other strong, negative feelings.

In response, Drew develops the theme Wild and Tame. The goal of the theme is to help the children gain a clearer understanding of the concept of control and of their feelings and needs related to it. To accomplish the goal, Drew introduces several new and varied activities that promote the use of HOT skills in the process of exploring wildness/tameness and out of control/control. These include reading and discussing relevant books, inventing stories, and using the stories as the basis for imaginary play scenarios that expand and add complexity to the stories.

During these activities, Drew jumps on the opportunities they present to engage children's higher-order thinking by asking incisive questions during discussions. Among the books they read and discuss are *Where the Wild Things Are* (Sendak 1963), *The Lion and the Mouse* (Pinkney 2009), and *No, David!* (Shannon 1998) and a few other books in the David series.

Drew leads the children through a process for making up a story called "Chain Stories" (which is described later in this chapter on page 138). One of the stories they create is about a tiger who is captured for the circus and is tamed and taught tricks to perform in a circus act. She misses her home and her family, but it takes several years and a few failed escape attempts before she has an opportunity to escape and return home. During those years, she had become a star of the circus with her amazing tricks. She is happy to be home and reunited with her family, but it doesn't take long before she feels restless and bored. Life at home is a lot less exciting than the circus—there is no one to appreciate her tricks—and now she misses all her human and animal friends. Finally, she makes a deal with the circus manager that she will return to the circus if she can perform for half of the year and spend the other half of the year at home.

Drew asks the children probing questions that initiate (guided) discussions: "Can a real animal be both wild and tame? What would that look like? Can a person be wild? Tame? Describe a wild person. A tame person. What might cause a person to be wild? Can a wild person be tamed? How? Can a person be both wild and tame? What would that look like?" As the children act out the story and improvise on the plot, Drew observes carefully for changes to their thinking about control, the aspects of control that they focus on, and any new concerns that might emerge.

Common themes in pre-K and kindergarten programs, such as transportation, community workers, winter (and other seasons), and Thanksgiving (and other holidays), lend themselves more to LOT skills than HOT skills. In situations where teachers are required to use themes like these, they can be made more effective by incorporating them under a broader HOT theme. For example, the theme Changes can incorporate the topic of seasonal changes, highlighting winter. Activities can involve differentiating changes among seasons, determining the cause of seasonal changes (connecting causes and effects), investigating how the changes are linked and circular (synthesizing and inducing), and how they impact children's lives (connecting causes and effects and generating ideas). Changes happen to everything in nature, including people. Just as the tilt of Earth over time—the year it takes to orbit the sun completely—causes the four seasonal changes, the course of time and events cause changes in people's lives. Births, marriages, divorces, and deaths change families. Turning five and starting kindergarten means changing schools, teachers, friends, and activities (and perhaps riding a school bus for the first time).

It can be challenging to develop activities that make the concepts addressed by HOT themes concrete, interactive, and understandable to young learners. It is an additional challenge to develop activities that also elicit higher-order thinking to deepen students' understanding of the concepts. Therefore, HOT themes should be planned well in advance so there is ample time to research the topic, develop effective activities, identify resources, and obtain quality materials.

Projects and Investigations: Inquiry in Action

Projects and investigations are inquiry-based learning strategies, which are ideal for implementing HOT themes and responding to questions and concerns. Inquiry-based learning offers great opportunities to integrate content area learning, observe the range of thinking styles among students, scaffold knowledge and abilities, and document students' efforts, problem-solving strategies, and changes in thinking through stories, photos, and videos.

Projects take place over an extended period of time and involve multiple related activities. Often, the activities contribute to the creation of a final product or set of products. Projects usually relate to the theme but can be done in parallel with theme-based projects in response to a significant and complex issue, concern, question, or problem.

An investigation is a shorter-term and less comprehensive strategy than a project, effective for answering certain questions or understanding a basic concept or idea. Investigations are processes for discovering the answer to a question and coming to an understanding of an idea. Being given an answer or explanation involves LOT skills (identifying and memorizing). Investigations engage higher-order thinking. Of course, not every question or idea can be, or should be, the subject of an investigation. But teachers can occasionally initiate short, mini-investigations by asking, "What do *you* think?" in response to questions and at the start of a brief explanation of an idea.

Projects and investigations are inquiry driven. They are flexible and open-ended processes, and very often the plans and activities, or even the original line of inquiry, change during the process in response to what is learned. Even when the final product of a project is planned in advance, exactly how it will turn out is not predetermined. The specific content or look of the product will be the result of the inquiry process.

Below are fuller descriptions of two projects previously referred to in the examples of HOT themes:

- This project for first to third graders involves the development of games as one strategy to implement the theme Luck Doesn't Last. There are four categories of games: those in which winning or losing is (1) entirely the result of luck, (2) mostly the result of luck and a little skill, (3) mostly the result of skill and a little luck, and (4) entirely the result of skill. Games can be of any type, such as board games, sports, video games, and so on. Students study existing games of different types that fit into each of the four categories. They work in groups to invent a set of four games of any type, one for each category. Alternatively, they can create one game with four sets of rules. Then they make the game or games, test them, revise them as necessary, and share their work during a whole-class family game night at the school.

- This project for second to third graders, about people who excel, is one strategy to implement the theme Good, Better, Best. Students work in groups to create multimedia presentations about a living person of their choosing who excels in some way and has achieved great things. It can be a famous person, such as an athlete, actor, musician, scientist, or artist. The presentation must focus on information about the person's childhood and background and the story of how they came to be accomplished (not famous). After each presentation, there is a guided discussion about the challenges and supports, the type and amount of effort, and the role of innate ability and other factors that contributed to the person's success. Then students do similar, but individual, presentations about someone they know or are related to. The teacher assists them to develop good questions for interviewing the person.

Through investigations, students experience basic research methods within activities appropriate for young learners. Research is our primary means of inquiry. Although it can be imperfect, wrong, misapplied, and sometimes faked, research has given us every piece of technology we have and every medicine we take and has taught us everything we know about ancient history, the cells in our body, and outer space. Two types of investigations are described below. The first one connects to the HOT theme No Fair! It addresses a common concern about claims of unfairness: "Is it really unfair, or does it just feel that way?" It uses social science opinion research methods. The second example connects to the HOT theme Brain Power and uses the literature review method of research adapted for young learners.

No Fair! An Investigation Using Social Science Opinion Research Methods

This investigation was initiated when a first-grade teacher overheard some of her students complain about having too much homework. They said that it isn't fair that they have more homework than their older siblings. The teacher agreed that it *is* unfair—if it is true. If the investigation finds that her students do have more homework than older students, she promises to reduce it. The investigation starts with formulating the following research questions:

- Do first graders have more homework than second and third graders?

- How much more (or less) homework do they have?

Next is the hypothesis (a type of inductive thinking/theorizing): "First-graders do have more homework, a half hour more than second graders and fifteen minutes more than third graders." Data collecting entails first graders asking all second and third graders how much time they typically spend doing homework every day. In addition, the teacher collects two weeks of homework assignments from the second- and third-grade teachers to count the number of daily tasks and their estimate of how long it should take students to complete them. The teacher tallies all results (calculating) with the students, explaining what she is doing and why (modeling) and involving them as much as possible. Then she leads them in creating a series of simple graphs to visualize the data (representing). After reviewing the data and doing a simple analysis (such as more/fewer, big differences/small differences/no differences, expected results/unexpected results), they could definitively answer the research questions, if only the bell hadn't rung to end the school day!

Brain Power: An Investigation Using Literature Review Research Methods

This investigation for preschoolers and kindergartners is to explore the concept of brain power (a HOT theme) in general and, more specifically, how it can be used to thwart or defeat physical power or danger, especially for a small person or animal. Research methods entail collecting and reviewing brain power ploys in stories and analyzing (a thinking process) and synthesizing the information (a creative thinking skill). Stories include fairy and folk tales, contemporary children's fiction and nonfiction books, newspaper and magazine articles (summarized and retold by the teacher), and personal stories from students' family members and from other teachers and staff in the school.

In the process of collecting all the brain power ploys, the teacher guides the children to look for commonalities among them. This naturally leads to categorizing them (a logical thinking skill). The teacher guides brainstorming sessions (generating ideas) and discussions after each reading to describe and make associations and differentiations among ploys (A/D thinking, a critical thinking skill). Identifying the categorizations is an ongoing process; they are added to and amended over the course of the investigation. The students come to realize that the ploys can be described in two main ways, by their type and by their purpose, although some ploys have more than one purpose and some are of more than one type. The four types of ploys are verbal (using words or sounds), physical (using the body or moving), visual (using small size as an advantage or using disguises), and assisted (using props or tools or getting the help of an ally). The three purposes are to avoid capture or danger, help others, and escape, defend, or protect themselves. This gives the teacher and the class a method and the vocabulary to make the concept of brain power more concrete and understandable.

To help the students synthesize the information, the teacher makes and posts a chart of the categorizations using symbols and graphics. As new examples arise, they use the chart to associate and differentiate them from other ploys with similar characteristics. They play a simple game in which the teacher describes a conflict or a dangerous or scary situation (some are fantastical and some are plausible) and, referring to the chart, challenges the students to use their brain power to get out of it safely and peacefully. When appropriate, they act it out. The students also challenge the teacher with scary situations (many seem to involve dinosaurs), which are great opportunities for the teacher to model brain power.

Materials That Matter

Most commercially made single-purpose materials are like LOT skills: functional and necessary, but limited. These include common useful instruments like scissors, staplers, rulers, pens, and paper, as well as classroom materials such as puzzles, manipulatives, table games, most software/apps, and books. For these classroom materials, it is necessary to have multiple versions at varying levels of difficulty. This meets the needs of the range of students' ability levels and interests in a typical class and provides the means for students to progress and develop and improve HOT skills. A preschooler who finds a ten-piece puzzle challenging at the start of the year may be able to complete a thirty-piece puzzle by the end of the year. A first grader who struggles to read *Green Eggs and Ham* in September may be reading *How the Grinch Stole Christmas!* by Christmas. Throughout this book are examples of teachers using children's books to promote higher-order thinking. The use of all the materials discussed in this section—loose parts, Crayon Physics (software), game cards, and others—should not be limited to structured activities. Students at all grade levels need ample time to use them freely and explore their possibilities. Observing students in self-directed activities and play provides teachers with important information about children's thinking and with natural opportunities to develop or expand students' HOT skills and teach new knowledge.

Loose Parts

Loose parts are groups of similar items that have no specific function and can be used in unlimited ways. These can range from small items such as beads and shells of various kinds and collections of plastic caps to large items such as wooden boards and boxes of various sizes for use outdoors. Loose parts can also be materials that can be manipulated, such as wire, string, clips, straws, ribbons, and cloth. Loose parts unleash higher-order thinking. They give students ample and rich opportunities to explore the physical qualities of the materials; categorize, sequence, and pattern them in many ways; make representational or free-form structures; create imaginary scenarios; invent games; and much more. And they give teachers many tools to create challenging and enjoyable activities, planned and spontaneous, that promote a wide range of HOT skills.

Loose parts often consist of items from nature that are aesthetically pleasing to the eyes, nose, and hands, such as sticks, leaves, seedpods, shelled nuts, and the stones used in the *ThinkinGame* Game of Stones, on pages 40–41. Repurposed inexpensive mass-produced items, which make valuable art, craft, math, and science materials for promoting HOT skills, include colored plastic drinking straws, ice cream sticks, beads, marbles, paper clips and clothespins of different colors, string, rubber bands, wire, pipe cleaners, wood scraps, screws, nuts and bolts, ribbon, buttons, and fabric. Commercially produced products with loose parts, or "sets," are mostly construction toys (interlocking plastic bricks and wooden unit blocks) or math manipulatives (connecting cubes and attribute shapes). Sets nicely complement loose parts, so it is good to have both. Sets provide consistent and sturdy items with specific useful functions, particularly for representational and logical tasks, but with limited purposes and uses. Loose parts have almost unlimited purposes and uses but can be ephemeral and not always useful for representational and logical tasks.

Arranging and displaying loose parts so they are visually attractive, well organized, and easy to access and reshelf ensures they will be used often and cared for properly. Materials that support organizing, categorizing, creating, and inventing with loose parts include containers, boxes, and trays of various sizes, magnifying glasses, blank paper and markers, graph paper with large squares, dice, and game spinners. For more ideas, see Daly and Beloglovsky (2014).

Loose parts outdoors may consist of scrap materials or commercial products, or both. Scrap materials can include strong wooden boards of various lengths, sturdy wooden boxes of various sizes, rope, sheets, and tarps. Children can create anything they can imagine and use what they create for social-imaginative play (pretend play) scenarios or to give themselves physical challenges. Often, they are used in conjunction with more standard, unmovable playground equipment to provide stability to their structures. Commercial products are essentially big versions of construction toys. They can be large hollow wooden blocks (big blocks), plastic snap-together bricks, or sets of plastic tubes, pipes, and connectors.

Technology: A Lot of LOT, Not Much HOT

Computer hardware and utility software and apps can be great tools for teachers to facilitate HOT teaching. They can make learning lively and interactive, provide access to millions of resources and sources of information, preserve and display student work, and much more. But as tools for young learners, there is little that promotes higher-order thinking; most software engages and reinforces lower-order thinking. Many websites with resources for young learners are too visually busy, commercialized, and not designed for nonreaders or even beginning readers. A delightful exception is the New York Metropolitan Museum of Art's website MetKids (www.metmuseum.org/art/online-features/metkids). While focused on art and creativity, it also has information about history, geography, and "big ideas," including inventions, mythology, fashion, and sports, as seen through the lens of the artwork in the museum.

There are some open-ended art studio software programs and apps, but drawing with real markers, pens, and colored pencils and painting with watercolors and other media using real brushes are much better options for creative expression.

There are, nevertheless, two software programs/apps that are cleverly designed to promote higher-order thinking, including creative thinking: Crayon Physics and ScratchJr or, for older students, Scratch. Crayon Physics (http://crayonphysics.com) is a computer simulation game that somehow manages to engage and challenge both logical and creative thinking simultaneously. It is truly a *ThinkinGame*. On the purely graphic interface, the player is given a task such as pushing a ball off a tall platform so it will land on a shorter platform. The task is accomplished by drawing freeform shapes and lines that, when completed, move in space and interact, accurately following the laws of physics. As there are unlimited ways to accomplish each task, some of which are simple, the goal is to complete the task in a uniquely clever and creative way. The drawings can be done with a mouse or directly on a touch screen. Unlike art studio software, these activities can only be done on a computer. In addition, there are tasks at many levels of difficulty, so even preschoolers can use it and adults can be challenged. It is a commercial program but relatively inexpensive. This is a unique game and there is no other like it. Available since 2009, hopefully it will continue to be available far into the future.

ScratchJr, for five- to seven-year-olds (www.scratchjr.org), and Scratch, for ages eight and above (www.scratch.mit.edu), are programs that enable students to use code (symbols) to write computer programs to create simple games and interactive stories. Because the possibilities are almost limitless, they have a strong creative component, although of a different type than Crayon Physics. They emphasize logical thinking in the programming and inductive thinking for the content. Students need instruction and practice to use them, whereas they can start playing around with Crayon Physics almost immediately. Characters, actions, and typical computer commands (start or stop a script, repeat a command, loop back to the start) are represented by icons. Students sequence the icons to create their stories and games. Some of the commands indicate what the user needs to do (touch an object, input a number or letter), which allows students to create games. Scratch, for older students, is closer to a complete programming language. Both versions have abundant teacher resources, and both are free. ScratchJr and Crayon Physics are two examples of activities that put the power of technology into the hands of young learners and are equal parts enjoyable play and intellectually rigorous learning. Similar programs and apps that provide coding tools and practice for young learners include Tynker (www.tynker.com) for ages seven and up; Kodable (www.kodable.com) for ages five to eight; Code & Go Robot Mouse

Activity Set (www.learningresources.com) for ages five and up; and Pre-reader Express and other curricula from Code.org (www.code.org) for ages four to eight. Because technology changes rapidly, some of these resources may no longer be available and new ones will certainly be developed. Search for "coding for young learners" in your web browser to access the most current resources.

Handmade Materials: The Example of Math Playing Cards

Because teachers know the needs, interests, and abilities of their students, materials they develop on their own can be particularly useful and effective and will be well liked and well used by their students. Together, teachers and students can create items with multiple uses, like game spinners and dice of various types and levels of difficulty, generic game boards, and sets of lotto cards and math playing cards. Math playing cards have the same characteristics as standard playing cards but have no picture cards and the suits are shapes. The two suit colors are the same, black and red. Cards are referred to as "two of circles" or "twelve of rectangles." The cards should be slighter larger than standard playing cards, made with good-quality stiff card stock, and laminated so they will last.

Almost any game that can be played with standard playing cards can be played with math playing cards, plus many more. The highest value card in the partial set illustrated on page 129 is twelve so the complete set would have forty-eight cards, but higher value cards can be added in sets of four, one of each suit. Also a set of four cards with zero value can be added, as well as a set of "X cards." X cards are wild cards that can have any value the player chooses or represent a preestablished directive such as "multiply rather than add." This introduces the algebraic concept that X represents an unknown. It's also a good idea to make sets of cards with other suits, such as ellipses, rhombuses, pentagons, and hexagons. For younger learners, higher value cards can be removed. (The highest card can be five, for example.) However, more cards will need to be added because most games require more than twenty cards. There can be duplicate math cards, which are actually useful rather than problematic as with playing cards.

There are many other possible variations of math playing cards. The shapes on the cards can be randomly scattered or grouped in different ways. For example, the red nine cards can have four shapes in the top row, three in the middle row, and two in the bottom row, while the black nine cards could have the rows in reverse order. For seven- and eight-year-olds, a set of cards could just have the black and red number symbols with only one shape on each card to indicate the suit. Every classroom should have multiple sets of several versions so that several groups of

COUNTING CARDS SAMPLE

students can play at the same time and a range of ability levels can be accommodated. The game Twins, and its variations, which use these cards, is described later in this chapter on pages 134–135.

Play: From Playing with Props to Playing with Ideas

As preschoolers become early primary students and older, imaginary play (also called pretend play or dramatic play) gradually moves from mostly externalized corporeal play, like pretending to be a pirate or playing with pirate figures, to mostly internal mental play, like thinking about being a pirate, reading and talking about pirates, making up stories about pirates, and distinguishing pirate fact from fantasy (Saifer 2010; Vygotsky 1978). "Playing with ideas" is an expression that reflects this concept, and to play with ideas is to use HOT skills.

Play in Preschool

Social-imaginative play for preschoolers is not just a teaching strategy but an activity that teaches. According to developmental psychologist Alison Gopnik, "Children learn much more from using their own brains to just observe and play than they do by having someone sit down and teach them. . . . Play doesn't get you to be better at doing any one thing in particular, but it gives you more flexibility in doing many different things" (Lewis 2016). However, this is only true if teachers facilitate and mediate children's play to ensure it is productive, complex, and multifaceted. Facilitating complex play entails helping children develop play skills and providing an ample and diverse supply of dress-up clothes, props, and big blocks.

Curriculum developers Deborah Leong and Elena Bodrova (2012) wrote a detailed guide to help teachers facilitate and mediate increasingly complex levels of children's social-imaginative play. It includes the following schema that describes the sequential levels of complexity in relation to elements of complex play or, in their terms, mature play (see figure 10). The play involves planning, clearly delineated roles, the use of props (realistic, representational, imaginary), an extended period of time, extensive use of language, and a defined, flexible scenario (29). At the more advanced levels (stages four and five in the schema), there are few activities for preschoolers as mentally complex as social-imaginative play. It entails using many HOT skills, at least at a basic level. Children use their imaginations, interact socially with several children at once, use language to direct the course of the play, negotiate roles and scenarios (solve problems), take on the persona of a different person (shift perspective), create a story line (generate), use props in unique ways (imagine), move physically, and more.

FIGURE 10
LEVELS OF COMPLEXITY OF SOCIAL-IMAGINATIVE PLAY

	1. First Scripts	2. Roles in Action	3. Roles with Rules and Beginning Scenarios	4. Mature Roles, Planned Scenarios, Symbolic Props	5. Dramatization, Multiple Themes, Multiple Roles
Planning	Does not plan during play.	Does not plan during play.	Plans roles; actions are named prior to play.	Plans each scenario in advance.	Plans elaborate themes, scenarios, and complex roles. Spends more time planning than acting out the scenario.
Roles	Does not have roles.	Acts first and then decides on roles. No rules are revealed.	Has roles with rules that can be violated.	Has complex, multiple roles.	Can play more than one role at a time. Roles have social relationships.
Props	Plays with objects as objects.	Plays with objects as props. Actions with a prop result in a role.	Needs a prop for the role.	Chooses symbolic and pretend props.	Does not need props to pretend or stay in the role. Objects can have roles.
Extended time frame	Explores objects, but not play scenarios.	Creates scenarios that last a few minutes.	Creates scenarios that last 10–15 minutes.	Creates scenarios that last 60 minutes or longer. With support, can create scenarios that last over several days.	Creates scenarios that last all day and over several days. Play can be interrupted and restarted.
Language	Uses little language.	Uses language to describe actions.	Uses language to describe roles and actions.	Uses language to describe unfolding scenario, roles, and actions. Uses role speech.	Uses language to delineate the scenario, roles, and action. Book language is incorporated into role speech.
Scenario	Does not create a scenario. Can copy teacher's actions or follow teacher's directions, if script is simple and repetitive.	Creates a scenario that is stereotypical, with limited behaviors. Can incorporate modeled roles and actions, with support.	Plays familiar scripts fully. Accepts new script ideas.	Plays a series of coordinated scenarios that change in response to previous ones or the desires of players.	Same as Stage 4, but can also use themes from stories and literature.

Figure 10. Levels of Complexity of Social-Imaginative Play (Bodrova and Leong 2007)

Should teachers introduce content knowledge or promote HOT skills during imaginary play? Should teachers ask a student pretending to be a chicken farmer to count the number of imaginary eggs in the egg carton he is selling? The surprising answer is "No!" The teacher's role in children's imaginative play is to help them play at the most advanced level they are capable of, to help them get back on track when the play is "stuck" or disorganized, and to help them resolve conflicts. It is through play-based and playful *activities* that engage higher-order thinking that teachers should facilitate content knowledge. *ThinkinGames, Cognitivities,* investigations, and self-directed exploration with materials that matter are activities well suited for teaching content.

Beyond Preschool: Context-Based Learning

Time that four- to six-year-olds spend engaged in teacher-facilitated rich and complex imaginary play, as well as in exploratory play with materials that matter, is time spent forming the strong and flexible mental framework needed to construct more advanced and formal higher-order thinking structures. This construction process begins in earnest in first and second grades. The optimal method for building those structures efficiently and ensuring they will function and endure uses play-based and playful teaching and learning strategies. They cushion the mental effort required to apply HOT skills at increasingly advanced levels and to develop new HOT skills. Intellectual challenges are more enjoyable and engaging when presented through play or in playful ways. In addition, there is compelling research evidence that play-based strategies are more effective than direct instruction, particularly for learning for understanding (Bonawitz et al. 2011; Buchsbaum et al. 2011; Clements and Sarama 2014; Hirsh-Pasek et al. 2009; Weisberg, Hirsh-Pasek, and Golinkoff 2013).

Nonetheless, play-based teaching is a hard sell in the anxiety-ridden climate of accountability that pervades education today. To start, I suggest calling play-based strategies *context-based learning*, which is an accurate way to describe one of play's main properties. Play creates contexts that give meaning and purpose to learning. Other "serious" terms for the active learning that characterizes play are action research, exploration, experimentation, learning encounters, design testing, data collection, pilot testing, theory testing, applying theories of action, embedded content methodologies, and experiential learning. Of course, combining terms can make play sound even more "serious," such as "researching the application of game theory through context-based mathematical investigations!"

Most of the activities in this book are play based or, at the very least, are playful. The HOT themes, projects, and investigations previously discussed provide structures that support context-based (meaning play-based) learning. Following are ideas for games that promote a number of thinking skills and teach a range of content knowledge. There are also ideas for role plays and other strategies that are more akin to drama, which are well suited for kindergartners who, in spite of adults' (unrealistic) expectations for their behavior, still need to physically move, interact, talk, move again, and talk some more. While not all teaching and learning needs to be play based or playful, it is not difficult or time-consuming to add a few play elements or a bit of playfulness to an activity or task. A small amount of effort in this regard will have large educational benefits for students. There is also an important benefit for teachers—it makes teaching more enjoyable.

ThinkinGames

Games are terrific context-based teaching and learning strategies. And when they facilitate the acquisition of content knowledge with higher-order thinking, they are *ThinkinGames*. These interactive, enjoyable activities can potentially address any content area and facilitate the development of any and all MOT and HOT skills. *ThinkinGames* often require students to use two or more types of thinking at the same time or in quick succession. They also promote social skills, such as taking turns, and build executive function abilities, such as focused attention, self-control, persistence, and delayed gratification. When playing in teams, *ThinkinGames* can help students learn to collaborate.

While many games are competitive and losing can be difficult for some students, when they play games of different types often and regularly, they come to understand that everyone sometimes wins and sometimes loses, especially if there is any element of luck involved. This understanding can be further facilitated through the previously discussed themes, projects, and investigations that explore the concepts of luck, ability, practice, effort, and skill as they apply to winning.

Existing games can be modified, or new games can be created, that require students to use HOT skills in the process of playing. One quick way to modify games that involve points or numbers is to make a new rule that lower numbers beat higher numbers. Also, winning could mean having the fewest cards or no cards, having the lowest final score, or finishing last (outlasting one's opponent). Using such counterintuitive rules in games gives students practice applying HOT skills that can thwart thinking errors.

Game rules can change periodically, followed by discussions about the ways the changes impacted the game. Students can contribute ideas for changing rules (generative thinking) and predict what will happen (induce/theorize). Playing different types of games that use or require the same capabilities or strategies, or use the same game principles, helps students understand the strategies and transfer them to other activities (a critical thinking skill). For example, to wait and watch for an opportune moment is an important ability and effective strategy in many games. Skilled players have the patience to wait for a good pitch in baseball, a good card in a card game, a good opening to run back to the base in a game of tag, and a good opportunity to capitalize on an opponent's mistake. While patience may still be a virtue, there seem to be fewer and fewer exemplars of patience in popular culture for young learners to emulate. Another way to help students transfer concepts is to provide multiple variations of the same game, as in the example below.

THINKINGAME: TWINS

The basic version of Twins is the same as the card game War but uses math playing cards (as previously described on pages 128–130). For two players, the deck is divided in half with the cards face down. Players turn over the card on the top of their stack and place it face up on the table. The higher number card takes the trick. When the cards are the same number, they say, "Twins!" They place two more cards face down and play the third card. The player with the higher number card takes all four of their opponent's cards. If the deck includes duplicate cards, a hand could result in "Identical Twins." In this case three more cards are placed face down and the fourth card is played. The winner of the game is either the player with all the cards or the one with the most cards after a preset time period.

Twins Upside Down
In this variation, the lower value card beats the higher value card.

Twins: What's the Difference?
Players each overturn two cards and subtract the lower number from the higher number. The same numbers equal zero. The values of the difference determine the outcome. Before the game starts, or even before each hand, students decide if the higher value or the lower value difference wins the trick. A variation of this game entails playing three cards.

Twins: Limited Addition
This is the same game as Twins: What's the Difference? except card values are added together.

Twin Teams

There are two players on each team. The deck is divided into fourths. Each player overturns two cards, which are either subtracted (as in What's the Difference) or added (as in Limited Addition). Then the team members' resulting amounts are either subtracted or added. The team's results are then played against the other team. Using a large deck or two decks will make the game last longer.

Twin Teams Plus

Each player picks up two cards from the deck. The two team members look at the four cards together without revealing them to the opposing team. They arrange the four cards into two sets of pairs that will give them the best chances to win the next two hands. They put the cards back on their stacks so that the pairs they created will be played correctly. This process repeats after the two hands are played. The game can also be played with each player picking up three cards and strategizing the next three hands.

Twins II

Twins II is a different version of Twins, not just a variation. Except for Twin Teams Plus, winning is a matter of luck in the previous variations of Twins. Twins II introduces strategy (a thinking process), although luck still plays a major role. Each hand begins with the players looking at the card they pick up from the top of their stack without showing it to their opponent. Right away, they have a decision to make (another thinking process): play the card or "take a chance." If they both choose to play the card, the game proceeds as usual. Players would do this if they have a high number card because they are likely to win (if the rule is that the highest value wins). But, if their card is a low number, they could improve their chances of winning the hand by playing the next card on their stack. However, this risks the possibility of losing both cards. Here's how it works: While both players are holding their cards, Player A says, "Take a chance" because he holds a three of circles. Player B holds a ten of squares and so says nothing. They both place their cards face up on the table. (If Player B's card number was the same or lower, the game would proceed as usual.) Because Player B's card number is higher, Player A turns over the top card on his stack and plays that card. If Player A loses (for example, the next card is a five of triangles), both cards go to Player B and the decision to take a chance does not pay off. Of course both players can choose the "take a chance" option. Twins II can have all the same variations as Twins.

The following game can use words from any content area. It's a fun way to reinforce new vocabulary and concepts. In the example, the content area is natural science.

THINKINGAME: DON'T SAY THE WORD!

This game is played between two teams of five to six players, although it could be played with more. The teacher shows a picture or an actual item from nature to one student from Team A so that others on the team cannot see it. This student is called the "scholar." The scholar's task is to describe the item without using its name, while her teammates try to guess what it is (infer, induce, interpret/synthesize). This is timed with a stopwatch. If the scholar says the name of the item or her team does not guess it in a minute and a half, they are done and Team B has a turn with a different item from nature. (Teachers may need to adjust the amount of time per turn so it is optimal for their students.) The same rules apply to Team B. The team that guesses soonest gets one point. If both teams are not able to guess correctly, the item is revealed and no points are scored. The game continues with two different students, one from each team, taking the role of the scholar. The team with the most points after every student has a turn being the scholar is the winner. Pictures can be of a bird, a bird's nest, a tree, any forest or jungle animal, a river, a mountain, a waterfall, and so on. Items from nature can be a leaf, a stone, a flower, an acorn (or other seedpod), an apple (or other fruit), a nut, and other small items.

This game has the additional advantage that it requires few materials. In fact, it can be played with no materials at all. There are many variations to make the game more challenging as students become adept at playing it. Students who can read can be given a word rather than a picture or an item. Students can guess things that are more abstract, such as characters from a story, emotions, and activities such as writing, cooking, swimming, and singing. Activities that are specific are even more challenging, such as waiting for a bus, going on a family vacation, planting a vegetable garden, and, for a mind-bending challenge, playing Don't Say the Word! The word can be a content area concept such as gravity, verbs, the equator, respect, atoms, democracy, and so on.

The next game is noncompetitive. In fact, it's all about collaboration and communication. Nonetheless, it is one of the more challenging games in the book. It is a game that requires a great deal of practice and teacher assistance at first, but it is well worth the effort. Once they have achieved a reasonable level of competence, students will enjoy playing this game independently and experimenting with variations.

THINKINGAME: DESCRIBE IT/DRAW IT

Two students sit opposite of each other at a table. Each of them has paper and a pencil. In between them is a barrier so they cannot see the area of table in front of their partner. One partner starts by drawing a number or a letter on his paper. Then he instructs his partner how to draw it, making sure not to say the name of the number or letter (shift perspective). The instructions should be as specific and detailed as possible. Gesturing is highly discouraged! The partner draws on her paper following the directions she is being given (infer, interpret). When completed, she states the name of the number or letter. Then they take down the barrier to determine if it is correct. If it is not, they discuss the process and try to determine what went wrong (analysis). (This part of the game may require support from the teacher.) Then they switch roles and repeat the activity. The objective is to get as many correct in a row as they can, which is their "connection score." Teachers help partners keep track of their connection scores so they can try to best them. A student can be a member of several partnerships.

As students begin to master the game, it can be made more challenging. Drawings can have double-digit numbers, two letters, or short words. In one version of the game, all the numbers and letters are written and described as they appear upside down. Additional challenges can entail using mirror image versions of letters and numbers, common shapes, then uncommon shapes, then multiple shapes, then intersecting shapes.

The following language- and literacy-focused game is also noncompetitive and collaborative. There are no teams and no scores. The fun is in imagining and empowering the collective imagination of the class.

THINKINGAME: CHAIN STORIES

The teacher starts the story by describing a compelling situation or event and modeling formal, literary language. The topic could be related to a theme or a content area. The opening lines establish the main characters and set the plot in motion. Then students systematically take turns contributing to the plot; significant contributions, such as plot twists or new characters, are encouraged. The teacher guides the students with questions as needed. "What is most likely to happen next?" "What could happen that would be surprising? Or funny? Or helpful?" "What do you hope will happen?" "Is there another option?" The teacher may also need to help students maintain the tone of the story, to offer ideas that are plausible within the context of the story, and to provide sufficient details.

As a follow-up activity, the story can be recorded and/or key plot elements written down so it can be made into a class book. This will most likely require heavy editing first. Literary conventions like flashbacks, subplots, a narrator, and cliff-hangers can be gradually introduced to increase the challenge of the activity and teach new writing skills.

Listed below are the *ThinkinGames* that have been described in previous chapters:

- The Art of Lotto, on pages 26–27, focuses on associating and differentiating and addresses art and cultural knowledge.

- Conductor, on page 30, focuses on representational thinking and addresses music and geometry.

- Game of Stones, on pages 40–41, focuses on categorizing and deductive thinking and addresses natural science and language.

- Shape Shifting, on pages 58–59, focuses on imaginative thinking and addresses math.

- Family Groups, on pages 62-64, focuses on inductive/theoretic thinking and can address any content area.

- Rhyme Time, on pages 116–117, focuses on creative thinking and addresses language and literacy.

Crayon Physics, on page 127, is a commercial computer simulation game that focuses on creative and logical thinking. It addresses physical science and technology.

ScratchJr, on page 127, is a free app that enables young learners to code and focuses on creative and logical thinking. It addresses math and technology.

Case Studies

Case studies are not just for Harvard Business School students. They are as effective for third graders as they are for grad students. Case studies are short descriptions of real-life situations or dilemmas that are meaningful and relevant to young learners. Typically, students work in small groups to create responses or solutions. Case studies engage creative thinking because they do not have one answer or a correct answer. Topics range from a new student entering the class who is on the autism spectrum to responding to a rumor that the school will be closing. Case study work elicits logical thinking, such as connecting causes and effects, and creative thinking, such as inductive thinking, and synthesizing. The *Cognitivity* below is challenging, but it deals with an issue that is relevant and compelling to young learners.

COGNITIVITY: THE CASE OF THE UNKNOWN BULLY

Someone is bullying the kindergartners and first graders on the playground and in the neighborhood. No one is willing to say who the bully is because the bully threatens to beat up anyone who tells. The bully knows what the kindergartners and first graders are saying and doing, so there must be a few of them that inform the bully in exchange for being on the bully's good side. No teacher or parent has been able to catch the bully in action.

What is the best way to solve this problem? Students try to come up with several solutions and then choose the one they think is best. For a solution to be considered among the best, no one can get hurt and the bullying behavior should stop permanently. If the mean behavior can be transformed into kind behavior, that would be even better. The bully cannot be expelled or somehow removed from the school and neighborhood. Students are reminded that the bully does not necessarily have to be identified or dealt with directly, that the bully could be a boy or a girl, and to think about why someone would bully another person.

Mental Flossers

Mental flossers are quick, fun mental challenges. They are great for recharging between lessons or during transitions in preschools. Unlike nearly all the other strategies, mental flossers are not used for teaching content or to connect to a theme. This is intentional, as they are exercises for the mind, the way recess or outdoor play is exercise for the body. Some will require a few minutes of preparation between the end of the school day and the beginning of the next day. They engage a variety of HOT skills and can be easily modified to be more or less challenging. Students can work on the solutions to mental flossers individually, in pairs, or in small groups. Here are some examples:

- Identify two things in the room that are similar but not the same. This could be modified to identify as many things as possible that are all similar but not the same, or as many pairs of similar things as possible.

- Identify something in the room that was not here yesterday. For a greater challenge, the something can be intangible, such as sunlight, excitement, quiet, order, a science lesson, or comfort (room temperature).

- Identify something that is missing from the room today that was there yesterday. Hints can be given to make it easier.

- Identify three things in the room that are all different shades of the same color. For a greater challenge, think of something *not* in the room that is a fourth shade of the same color.

- What can be changed in the room (without adding anything) that would make it prettier? Safer? Friendlier? Cozier?

Preschoolers can find or locate the items rather than identifying them. For many of these tasks, students can work in pairs or small teams. Teachers adjust the level of difficulty so that most students are challenged but can still understand the task and not feel too frustrated. Mental flossers should become more challenging as the year progresses and students become more adept. Another level of challenge can be added for first and second graders and some kindergartners to engage additional HOT skills: students can think up mental flossers for other students and the teacher. Trying to stump the teacher with really hard challenges is something students will enjoy.

Role Plays and Sketches

As previously mentioned, these context-based learning activities are particularly well suited for kindergartners, although they are also effective and enjoyable activities for older students. If simple and straightforward, they can also work for some preschoolers. In role plays and sketches, students improvise the actions within the structure established by the teacher. Role plays help students gain a deeper understanding of ideas and concepts. They also give students practice using new skills, behaviors, and vocabulary to apply their newly acquired HOT skills in a variety of situations and contexts (transferring). Good examples of this are role plays that focus on resolving a conflict. Students practice applying HOT skills—generating ideas, evaluating, and shifting perspective—to resolve common conflicts set in playful and sometimes fantastical situations. Some role plays for resolving conflicts could be

- negotiating turns for taking the class Tyrannosaurus Rex (a.k.a. the teacher) for a walk;

- sharing equally the leftover half of an apple pie among three ants at a picnic;

- developing a process to decide which two of four astronauts will get to go to the moon; or

- determining how all the dogs in the pack can respond to the bossy and mean dog who won't invite them to her birthday party if they don't give her all their dog food.

Sketches are more prescriptive than role plays and involve more sophisticated improvisation, so they are better suited to seven- and eight-year-olds. Sketches start with a scene from a fiction book students are reading (or being read to) or from a nonfiction biography or story from history that students are studying. Students are assigned to play the characters from the book or the people involved in the event. Additional characters can be added to include more students in the sketch, as long as the roles are plausible and contribute to or do not detract from the story. By including nonspeaking roles, students who are introverted or who are learning English may be more willing to participate. The sketch begins with students acting out the scene as accurately as they can, but without a script. Of course, the teacher provides scaffolds as needed. Then they are encouraged and supported to improvise and expand the story or to go into more depth. Changing what actually happened is perfectly acceptable, as long as students are intentional about the changes and the changes are plausible. Almost any content area can be addressed in a sketch. With practice, young learners can become surprisingly adept at performing sketches.

Conclusion

Making meaningful choices, collaborating with classmates, using materials that matter, and learning through play, games, projects, and investigations that connect to important themes provide a diversity of significant and engaging opportunities for students to learn and practice the full range of higher-order thinking skills. While each of these strategies can be effective in and of itself for promoting the development of students' higher-order thinking, using all of them often and regularly over time increases the effectiveness of each one and infuses higher-order thinking throughout the curriculum.

Over time and through many varied experiences, a carpenter's apprentice learns much more than skills. She gains an understanding and appreciation of the unique qualities of each type of wood ("a feel for wood") and of each specialized tool ("a feel for tools"). She begins to internalize "a feel for the work" by seeing "intuitive expertise" applied to prevent and solve problems and to achieve the optimal balance of precision and creativity (Kahneman 2011). In the same way, students learn more than knowledge from teachers who promote higher-order thinking. They begin to get a feel for learning for understanding, for looking beyond surface appearances, and for doing intellectual, challenging work.

With the information in this chapter, and plenty of practice, teachers will be well equipped to make optimal use of all the higher-order thinking tools. To be fully equipped, however, requires knowing how to take full advantage of the opportunities that these general strategies provide. This entails the use of more specific strategies, or techniques, that directly elicit HOT skills.

Key Ideas from This Chapter

HOT strategies are general teaching strategies that assist teachers to develop their students' higher-order thinking skills. HOT strategies include the use of the following:

- social or cooperative learning strategies
- theme-based approaches that involve meaningful and challenging theme ideas

- project-based learning and investigations

- carefully selected and developed materials, including indoor and outdoor loose parts, certain computer programs/apps, and homemade games with multiple variations to challenge all students

- play-based and playful activities

- *ThinkinGames*, or games that promote higher-order thinking while teaching content

- case studies that provide students with a relevant, realistic problem to solve

- quick mental puzzles, called *mental flossers*, to recharge young minds

- activities that get students moving and using their whole bodies while practicing higher-order thinking through improvisational role plays and sketches

Questions for Discussion

- What can teachers do to ensure that when students work cooperatively and collaboratively, they will be effective and have a positive experience? How can teachers prevent or intervene effectively with typical group dynamics problems such as students who dominate, who don't participate or pull their weight, who pull others off task, who argue too much, and so on?

- Discuss various ways that technology, including cell phones, tablets, and video game players, can be used to promote higher-order thinking.

- In addition to using the term *context-based learning* for play-based strategies, what are other ways you can convince skeptics that play and playfulness are effective educational approaches?

- What are other potentially good topics or issues for case studies that will be relevant and engaging to young learners?

- What are other potentially good topics for role plays and sketches?

HOT Techniques for HOT Teaching:
Intentional *and* Playful

In the previous chapter, we used the analogy of hardware tools to explain that there are general strategies for applying the guiding principles. For cutting tools, the general strategy for applying the guiding principle "Check that the tool is in good working order before using it" was to determine if the blade needs to be sharpened or replaced. However, there are techniques for sharpening blades that are more efficient and effective than others and will greatly improve the chances of getting the desired result. And some types of blades require particular sharpening techniques. Using the wrong technique is inefficient and more likely to produce no result (it's still dull), a partial result (it's a little sharper), or a negative result (it's damaged).

In the same way, the techniques described in this chapter are most effective for sharpening students' HOT skills in general, and some are designed to sharpen particular HOT skills. These HOT techniques are at the level of teacher-student interactions, giving teachers some specific ways to develop students' HOT skills within the framework of HOT strategies, such as *ThinkinGames*, projects, and role plays. HOT techniques, individually and collectively, bring intentionality to the task of promoting and improving students' HOT skills. Because building the thinking skills to engage in intellectually rigorous learning is a long, slow, deliberate, and effortful process, it needs to be facilitated, guided, and supported with a high degree of intentionality. This is particularly important for teachers of young learners, who are in a position to build on their students' nascent hardwired thinking abilities and to "grease the skids" for the ever more complex cognitive challenges to come.

Choices

Offering many different kinds of choices many times a day provides the opportunities young learners need in order to learn to make good choices. Using HOT skills when choosing makes it a more deliberate and intentional choice and can provide new insights, understanding, and appreciation in the process. Choosing, which is a simple form of decision making, does not necessarily require higher-order thinking. Most of the time, inconsequential choices—the choice between riding the orange bike or the green bike—can and should be made quickly and without evaluating or using other HOT skills. Nonetheless, sometimes inconsequential choices are made with faulty or automatic thinking, and learning to use HOT skills to make intentional choices quickly is a great benefit and can lead to additional learning opportunities, as illustrated in the following *SnapsHOT*.

SNAPSHOT: ORANGE IS THE NEW GREEN

Nora (teacher): Reyna, I noticed that you seem to always choose the green bike and never the orange bike.

Reyna: Orange makes me think of Halloween and scares me. Green is like trees and grass. It makes me happy.

Nora: That is so interesting. Orange makes me think of fresh orange juice and makes me happy. Green makes me think of monsters and slimy things and scares me! (*Nora is doing a bit of strategizing to challenge Reyna's somewhat constricted thinking.*)

Reyna: (*laughing*) Really? Maybe I'm going to try thinking about orange juice instead of . . . you know what. But I think it's hard to do. (shift perspective)

Nora: Did you ever ride the orange bike, Reyna? You might like it because it's newer and a little bigger than the green one—more your size. There may be more important things about bikes than their color. And that's also true for many other things, like shoes and even people!

Reyna: Does it go faster? If it's faster, I'll ride it. (generate ideas)

Nora: See, there *is* something that's more important to you than the color! Well, it might be faster. It doesn't have a rusty chain like the green bike.

Reyna: Why is it rusty?

Nora: Over time, water will cause metal things to rust. I guess we left it out in the rain too many times. *(They look closely at the chain.)* See how rust makes metal rough and bumpy? The rusty bumps cause the chain to wobble more and weigh more than a smooth chain with no rust, which makes it harder to turn with the pedal. So it will probably be easier to make the orange bike go fast than to make the green bike go fast.

Reyna: But I still think I won't ever really, really like it . . . like an orange bike. Can I paint it? (A/D, generate, and reframe)

Nora: *(laughing)* While you ride it, I'll think about it.

In this *SnapsHOT,* the teacher subtly corrects the student's thinking errors. Reyna appears to believe that speed is an inherent quality of a bike (inherence heuristic). Nora reframes Reyna's thinking error when she explains that the pedal turns the chain and a chain that is easier to turn makes it easier for the rider to make it go faster. She communicates the concept that variations of speed are the result of differences in the qualities of particular parts of a bike combined with the volition of the rider.

Teachers of young learners give them a wonderful gift by helping them develop the habit of making considered choices rather than arbitrary, instinctive, or reactive ones. Knowing why one is making a particular choice and having the skills to make it thoughtfully but without too much deliberation is an important life skill with many potential benefits. To develop the habit of choosing thoughtfully, students need many opportunities to practice making many types of choices. Most students will also need some level of instruction, guidance, and scaffolding to use HOT skills and use them effectively when making choices.

Younger students should be given fewer and more limited choices than older students, and all choices should be age appropriate and feasible. All students should be challenged to advance their current level of thinking in regard to choosing.

Giving students choices should be the default mode for assignments, daily routines, and activities. Rather than all of the students in a reading group (or the whole class) reading the same book, they can be given a choice between reading either a fiction or a nonfiction book, both of which have been selected by the teacher to ensure they are appropriate and engaging. This provides the opportunity to hear students' discussions and arguments and scaffold their basic decision-making thinking skills. Kindergartners can choose between investigating the causes and consequences of earthquakes or hurricanes. Preschoolers can choose which song to sing at morning circle.

Choices made as a whole class or by groups of students are very valuable exercises but can be time-consuming (see the voting activity May the Best Map Win, on page 77). So, teachers need to give individual students opportunities to make choices for the group. A turn-taking chart ensures that all students get the same number of opportunities to make a choice. To create the chart, list all students' names vertically on a sheet of paper and attach it to a clipboard. Move a small black binder clip down the list of names to determine who will be next to have a turn to choose for the group. When the last student on the list has had a turn, move the binder clip back to the top. If a student is absent, put a small red binder clip next to the name and move the black one down to the next name. This serves as a reminder to give a turn to the student who was absent at the first opportunity.

Students at every grade level need time to engage in self-selected activities. For preschool it should last at least an hour; for kindergarten, forty minutes; for first grade, thirty minutes; and for second and third grades, twenty minutes. Students should be given a number of activities from which to choose, including playing small-group games, reading for pleasure, using creative art materials and open-ended construction materials, creating sketches, and engaging in complex social-imaginative play.

Scaffolds for Higher-Order Thinking

Scaffolding simply means helping students act or think more effectively, thoroughly, deeply, or at a slightly higher developmental level than they can on their own. When they no longer require assistance, the teacher removes the scaffold or continues the process by raising it a little higher. Scaffolds can be verbal, nonverbal, physical, or material. They can range from an encouraging nod and smile, to nonverbal and verbal cues, to offering suggestions, to asking HOT questions, to giving physical assistance, to providing materials. Any of these can be used to prompt higher-order thinking. The critical scaffolding skills for teachers are (1) to scaffold just above students' current level of ability, knowledge, and thinking and

(2) to give students only as much help as is necessary. Scaffolding is a very useful and effective all-purpose technique. It is a key strategy for individualizing and promoting all aspects of development, thinking, and learning.

Opportunities to scaffold HOT skills to great effect are plentiful during discussions, small-group activities, *ThinkinGames*, *Cognitivities*, projects, and investigations; when students are engaged with materials that matter; when teachable moments arise; and when helping students solve problems (like resolving conflicts), make decisions, analyze, and plan (the four key thinking processes).

The *SnapsHOT* below, an amusing anecdote of scaffolding children's investigation work, was written by Luke Touhill (2012, 3) and reprinted with permission from Early Childhood Australia.

SNAPSHOT: HOW TO DRAW A MIRROR

As part of a project that involved turning a cardboard box into a car, a group of children set themselves the task of making the car's mirrors. At first, it seemed simple, but as they started to work, it quickly became apparent that a mirror is actually a very difficult thing to draw. How do you capture the changing nature of reflection in a static image? It took most of the morning, plenty of animated discussion, and many trips to the bathroom to look at actual mirrors to arrive at an acceptable solution. As the morning progressed, the children discussed and tried various ways of representing a mirror. Much of this discussion was self-generated but, as the educator with the group, I took the role of following what was going on and asking questions that either extended children's thinking or helped to break a deadlock when they were stuck. Without the pressure of time or the need to come up with an instant solution, we could explore questions such as "What does a mirror do?" and "How does a mirror work?" At one point, the children were leaning towards finding something reflective to cover the mirror pieces with. Foil was considered but ultimately rejected because, while it was shiny, it just wasn't reflective enough. In the end, it was agreed that when you look in the mirror you see . . . yourself!

And so our car's mirrors became a series of self-portraits as each of the children drew pictures of themselves looking out from each of the mirrors.

In this case, finding the "right" solution wasn't crucial. Foil would actually have worked effectively, as would drawings of the cars or road behind. What was important was the thinking that went into arriving at the ultimate solution. While it was challenging for the children, it was also absorbing and interesting. There was genuine intellectual effort for each of the children involved in grappling with the idea of drawing a mirror, and the sense of accomplishment when they hit upon an idea that suddenly seemed right for everybody was an important validation of the process.

The teacher scaffolded the children's problem-solving and decision-making skills (thinking processes) and the HOT skills of generating, representing, and inducing/theorizing. He did this by asking incisive questions, suggesting they look at actual mirrors to examine their properties, and providing a variety of resources and materials such as foil. The children most likely rejected using the foil, which many adults would see as a good choice, because their examinations and discussions led them to conclude that a mirror is defined by what it does, reflect images, not by its appearance, however shiny and silvery.

Cues

Cues are reminders. They are a type of heuristic, or shortcut, for quickly jogging a student's memory. Cues are used to remind students to use a HOT skill and to help them use it effectively. Cues minimize the disruptions to discussions and activities that happen with fuller explanations. Cues can be nonverbal (gestures), verbal, visual, or some combination of the three. Visual cues use simple graphics or symbols and can elicit certain HOT skills directly. They are a form of representational thinking (all cues represent more complex ideas) and require students to infer their meaning and how to respond, at least at first, as responses to cues tend to become automatic after a while. Below are some examples of cues. These are suggestions, which teachers should freely change or adapt as needed to be more responsive to their students' learning needs and thinking styles.

Nonverbal (Gestural) Cues

- Both hands on head, serious facial expression: Use higher-order thinking.
- Time-out sign followed by both hands on head, serious facial expression: Stop and use higher-order thinking.

- Index fingers of both hands pointing at temples, serious facial expression: Use deep thinking (critical thinking).

- Index finger on lips, head slightly tilted, eyes looking up and to the left, whimsical facial expression: Use creative thinking or imagine.

Visual Cues

Visual information in the form of computer icons, emoticons, and all those universal symbols for recycling, accessible parking, restrooms, elevators, and others have become a common form of communication in our world. Many of them are visual cues that guide behavior: where to park, where not to park, where to go to claim your bags at the airport, where your old newspapers can be recycled, and where to find the waiting room in at the hospital. Simple, clear, easily understood graphics are also effective teaching materials for helping students, particularly nonreaders, remember the meaning and purpose of a concept and for guiding students' behaviors, including their thinking.

Each thinking skill can be represented by a simple graphic that suggests its meaning or function. Here are a few ideas:

- logical thinking skills

- calculate

- connect causes and effects

- represent

- critical thinking skills

- associate/differentiate

- shift perspective

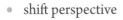

- evaluate

- creative thinking skills

- imagine

- generate

Verbal Cues

Verbal cues are very short, quick reminders; otherwise, they would be directions.

- Take your time.

- Don't hurry.

- Think slowly/deeply/through to the end.

- Use higher-order thinking/deep thinking/creative thinking.

- Avoid thinking errors / faulty thinking.

- Dig deep.

- Imagine . . .

- Play with it.

- Run with it.

- Have fun with it.

- Keep an open mind.

Modeling/Demonstrating

The art of modeling or demonstrating higher-order thinking is to do it so that students will transfer the information (a HOT skill) and not imitate it (a LOT skill). One good way to do this is to think out loud while using a HOT skill or a thinking process for tasks that are neither academic nor too commonly used by students. For example, to model decision making, a teacher might say, "I have to decide if I should wear my new coat when we go outside or leave it here. If I wear it and get too warm, I'll have to carry it. If I set it down outside, it will get dirty and I might forget it. But it's too cold to be without a coat . . . or something. Aha! I can take a sweater instead." Modeling, when done well, is an effective technique for teaching thinking skills explicitly, without being didactic or overly directive. This is particularly helpful for students with contextual thinking styles.

In the *SnapHOT* Why It's Hard to Explain Why, on page 82, the teacher models ways to respond to "why" questions. His goals are for students to learn the vocabulary that is commonly used to answer such questions and the various types of responses that are possible. This is a bit trickier than thinking out loud to promote transferring over imitation because the teacher is modeling HOT skills in the same academic task that he wants his students to do. However, he mitigates this problem by modeling his responses *after* students have given theirs.

There are many examples of modeling in the *SnapsHOT* Orange Is the New Green, on pages 146–147. This type of modeling is mostly implicit—the teacher uses HOT skills in her conversation with her student, although she occasionally uses explicit terms like *cause* and *effect*. While this eliminates the concern that students will imitate rather than transfer, its impact on students' thinking is indirect, long term, and hard to see or document. But the indirect, long-term positive effects of using implicit teaching can be widespread and powerful (Elango et al. 2016; Weiland and Yoshikawa 2013). Modeling HOT skills often and in many different ways is the best way to ensure that implicit teaching is also effective teaching.

In Orange Is the New Green, the teacher models reframing by responding to the student's negative assignation of orange and positive assignation of green by saying, "Orange makes me think of fresh orange juice and makes me happy. Green makes me think of monsters and slimy things and scares me!" She models transferring when she states, "There may be more important things about bikes than their color. And that's also true for many other things, like shoes and even people!" Connecting causes and effects and deductive thinking are modeled in the teacher's explanation of the causes of rust, the effects of rust on metal, the reason that rust makes it harder to turn the wheel with the pedal and the effect that has on how fast a bike can go. Finally, she models taking the time to think before making a decision when she says, "While you ride it, I'll think about it," in response to the student's request to paint the bike.

Idioms and Aphorisms

English is full of common expressions that reflect cultural values and shared wisdom. When teachers use these idioms or aphorisms (also called proverbs, sayings, expressions, words of wisdom), they help students develop HOT skills such as representing, associating and differentiating, evaluating, and transferring. Like cues, aphorisms and idioms are heuristics; most are similes, metaphors, or analogies that capture the essence of an idea or concept (a type of representational thinking). They help students develop, sharpen, and expand conceptual thinking in general. Like cues, they are used as reminders before an action ("Look before you leap!"), but they are also used to express an evaluation after an action (a critical thinking skill): "You know what they say, 'Look before you leap!'"

Idioms and aphorisms represent larger concepts or messages (a logical thinking skill), although not explicitly or directly. Implicit or indirect messages can be very powerful. Perhaps the most famous teacher in history, Plato knew this and so made extensive use of parables and analogies in his teaching. The implicit message of "Look before you leap!" is to be cautious and not impulsive and to plan and think ahead before acting, particularly before a bold or risky action. All of this in four words! The power of this aphorism, as with many others, lies in the combined effect of its brevity (a quality of all heuristics), its vivid imagery, and its implicitness. This is why these expressions are so widely known and used and have endured. Some can be traced back thousands of years.

When first introducing an aphorism, teachers should determine if students understand its message and, if necessary, help them uncover its meaning. One way to do this is to follow the saying with its explicit meaning or a more child-friendly version, trying to match its tone and cadence: "Don't count your chickens before they hatch" can be followed with "Don't assume you will have something before you have it." Or "Don't assume that things will work out perfectly or as you hope." Or "Don't invite friends to the victory party before you've won the game." But there is another significant reason to use aphorisms and idioms: many of them are about the importance of using higher-order thinking, particularly critical thinking and planning (a key thinking process).

Higher-Order Thinking in General

- Think before you act.
- Think before you speak.
- Before you assume, learn.
- Before you judge, understand.
- Be open minded.
- The pen is mightier than the sword.

Critical Thinking

- You can't judge a book by its cover.
- Beauty is only skin deep.
- There's more than meets the eye.
- All that glitters is not gold.
- Appearances can be deceiving.
- Dig a little deeper.
- Take it with a grain of salt.

- Read between the lines.
- Look behind the curtain.
- Scratch beneath the surface.
- Don't believe everything you see/hear/read.

Shifting Perspective

- The grass is always greener on the other side of the fence.
- One person's trash is another person's treasure.
- One person's ceiling is another person's floor.
- Beauty is in the eyes of the beholder.
- Don't judge people until you have walked a mile in their shoes.
- There are two sides to every coin.

Logical Thinking and Connecting Causes and Effects

- What goes up must come down.
- What goes around, comes around.
- Chickens come home to roost.
- Don't put the cart before the horse.
- You reap what you sow.
- Better safe than sorry.

Planning

- Hope for the best, prepare for the worst.
- The early bird catches the worm.
- Don't count your chickens before they hatch.
- Don't put all your eggs in one basket.
- Look before you leap.
- Don't miss the boat.
- You can't put the toothpaste back in the tube.
- Measure twice, cut once.

Inducing/Theorizing

- Connect the dots.
- Piece it together.

Creative Thinking

- Think outside the box.
- Think for yourself.
- The sky's the limit.
- Let your imagination run wild.
- Think big.
- Think the unthinkable.
- Expand your horizons.

Analogies, Similes, and Metaphors

In the English language, analogies, similes, and metaphors are so plentiful that we are often unaware of them. There are thousands of them that convey a wide range of messages and are common figures of speech. Some are particularly good for promoting higher-order thinking because they are so vivid, clever, poetic, or insightful.

- This (computer/car/phone) is a dinosaur.
- Life is a dance, not a race.
- They're like peas in a pod.
- It's like nails on a chalkboard.
- He's like a fish out of water.
- It's like a diamond in the rough.
- She's like a puppet on a string.
- That's music to my ears.
- He's still a bit green.
- She's the puppet master.
- He thinks he's the center of the universe.
- She's a peach.
- He's a rock.
- It's all just smoke and mirrors.

- It's a house of cards.

- It's a red herring.

- The horse is out of the barn.

- The train has left the station.

- Let's cross that bridge when we come to it.

- You can't get blood from a turnip.

And here's a recent one from child development research: "eating the marsh-mallow" (Mischel, Ebbesen, and Zeiss 1972), which means acting impulsively, succumbing to instant gratification, and not having enough self-control to wait for something better, even when you know it's a sure thing. The metaphor is usually expressed as "Don't eat the marshmallow!" or "He ate the marshmallow!"

If necessary, modify analogies slightly to help students understand them better or to make them more appropriate for young learners. "It's like putting a Band-Aid on a broken bone" is probably a better choice than the common version that puts the bandage on a bullet wound.

Making up analogies, similes, and metaphors that are relevant and under-standable to students models creative thinking, as well as the logical thinking skills of associating and differentiating, and representing. Characters from popular children's literature are good sources:

- "You are kinder than the lion who didn't eat the mouse!"

- "You two are the best friends since Frog met Toad!"

- "I got dirtier than Harry on a bad day!"

- "This room looks like David and Curious George had a party!"

- "How old am I? If I were a turtle, I'd be more Morla than Mutant Ninja."

Students can also do this. A good place to start is to think of new terms for common similes:

- Quiet as _____.

- Smooth as _____.

- Silly as _____.

- Deep as _____.

- Strong as _____.

- Sharp as _____.

HOT Questions: "Roses and Thorns"

Higher-order thinking questions facilitate learning for understanding by engaging HOT skills. A HOT question, being complex, often elicits multiple thinking skills and from more than one type (logical, critical, and creative thinking). There are two main types of HOT questions:

1. **Rose questions:** These are questions that reveal students' understanding, like sunlight reveals the many-petaled rose inside the bud. Rose questions simultaneously give teachers important information about how students think and help students think more intentionally. They nurture students' awareness of their own thinking processes and styles. Often, two or more rose questions are asked in a sequence to expose more layers of "petals." Rose questions might ask, "What more can you say about what happened? What else did you see? What did you do exactly? What is happening now? What do you think about the situation? How do you explain what is happening?"

2. **Thorn questions:** These are questions that challenge students' thinking. While they further reveal how students think, their main purpose is to provoke the use of new or more advanced levels of HOT skills in the process of learning. As "there are no roses without thorns," students' responses to rose questions inform thorn questions, and their responses to thorn questions inform rose questions. Thorn questions might ask, "What is the other side of the story? What might happen next and why? What are all the possible results? What can you change that would change the outcome? What is the worst that could happen? What is the best that could happen?"

The following *SnapsHOT* includes many examples of HOT questions (roses and thorns) as used by a preschool teacher to help a child solve an engineering problem. It also shows how she sequences HOT questions as part of the process of scaffolding the child's HOT skills for problem solving and for understanding certain concepts of physical science.

SNAPSHOT: GO WITH THE FLOW

Four-year-old Simon is as sharp as he is shy. As usual, he is by himself at the water table. He uses a small funnel to pour water from a beach pail into a clear plastic bottle with a narrow neck. Although the water goes neatly into the bottle, the funnel quickly fills and overflows. Seeing his frustration, his teacher, Nadia, helps him find solutions by sequencing HOT questions along with other scaffolding strategies.

Nadia: What do you want to happen, Simon?

Simon: The water to go in faster. To not spill.

Nadia: What makes that happen? What might cause it to spill?

Simon: I don't know. Maybe it just has to spill.

Nadia: Maybe. But if you do some higher-order thinking, I'm sure you can think of something to change or do differently that might stop the water from spilling. (*after a brief pause*) Any ideas?

Simon: Well, I can't change that (*pointing to the funnel*) because it's the only one.

Nadia: So are you saying that changing the funnel might fix it? You could be right. If we had lots of different funnels, which would you choose to fix it? How would it be different from this one?

Simon: Maybe a higher one than this fummel.

Nadia: Well, I see another funnel on the science table that looks like a bigger funnel, which probably means it's a taller funnel. You can get it and use it. Please ask for help when you need it. You don't ever have to be stuck!

(*Simon returns with the funnel.*)

Nadia: There is a saying, "If you don't ask, the answer is always no!" See, there was only one funnel, no other funnels . . . until you asked! What if that doesn't work? What can you do if the water still spills?

Simon: Is there more fum . . . funnels?

Nadia: I don't think so. But there are three other things you are using that you can change: the pail and the bottle are two things. We have lots of different bottles, cups, and containers to try. The third thing is the water.

Simon: I can change the water?

Nadia: In a way. You can change the way you pour the water: slower, faster, higher, lower, upside down, in a box with a fox!

Simon: In a house with a mouse!

Nadia: Exactly! So, I have a question. Which combination of pouring containers, funnels, filling containers, and ways of pouring will fix the spilling best? Would you like to investigate that question?

Simon: Okay.

Nadia: Take your time. Try many different combinations. When you are done, we can talk about it.

In the above *SnapsHOT*, the first question the teacher asks is, "What do you want to happen?" after seeing the child was struggling with something. The goal of the question is to get the student's perspective. It is not a HOT question but is intentionally worded to lay the foundation for the HOT questions to come.

The second set of questions she asks are rose questions: "What makes that happen? What might cause that to happen?" The answer would entail connecting causes and effects and using deductive and/or inductive thinking. The goal of these questions is to help the child think more deeply (critically) about the problem by connecting causes and effects. The teacher learns from the child's response that this is a sticking point. He says, "I don't know. Maybe it just has to spill." The questions may be too conceptual—a little beyond his comprehension. Or he may need help developing or improving cause and effect thinking as well as inductive and deductive thinking. To determine this, and at the same time continue the scaffolding process, the teacher asks a question that is contextual and includes directions for action.

She asks the child for his ideas for changing something that might stop the water from spilling, although it isn't in the form of a question exactly (which is only a problem on *Jeopardy!*). Embedded in this thorn question is a scaffold that helps the child focus his thinking on something he can change. Providing such supports along with a challenge is especially helpful to young learners. The teacher uses a very effective communication strategy. She indirectly communicates a positive assessment of the child's abilities, which is motivating and a boost to self-confidence. The question elicits generative thinking and connecting causes and effects, but, depending on the task, it can also elicit any other HOT skill and any number of combinations of HOT skills.

The child responds that he can't change the funnel because there are no others. This reveals that he had already developed a theory or hypothesis of the cause of the problem and how to solve it but believed he could not act on it.

His difficulty answering the previous questions was not because of weak conceptual thinking skills or an inability to connect causes and effects, but something else. Perhaps the question itself was too vague and unclear, not the concepts it represented. The reason he said, "Maybe it just has to spill" was revealed in this answer. He felt there were no options for changing the funnel. The student's difficulty solving problems, at least this problem, is due to factors that impact his ability to *apply* his good thinking skills—probably his shy personality. The teacher realizes this and reminds him to ask for help.

Then the teacher gives him an intellectual challenge, a thorn question, rather than a suggestion or directive to help him move forward. She asks him to mentally identify the attributes of a funnel that would be more effective: "If we had lots of different funnels, which would you choose? How would it be different from this one?" This HOT question elicits imagining, associating and differentiating, evaluating, and inducing.

An exchange follows in which the teacher assists, instructs, and provides content knowledge and a dose of playfulness. Then she asks another set of thorn questions: "What if that doesn't work? What can you do if the water still spills?" His response reveals that he sees the problem to be the funnel and nothing else. To move the process forward and set the stage for a question that will engage the child in an inquiry (this is also called a *spark*), the teacher provides information and instructions. As the inquiry will entail investigating many causes for an effect and multiple solutions for a problem, the teacher instructs him about the variables he can manipulate.

The final scaffold comes in the form of a very thorny question: "Which combination of pouring containers, funnels, filling containers, and ways of pouring works best?" This investigation will entail a good deal of hands-on connecting of causes and effects, associating and differentiating, deducing, inducing, synthesizing, and, undoubtedly, mopping! The same types and sequence of HOT questions are also effective for scaffolding K–3 students to work through any challenge in any content area.

Higher-order thinking questions are usually open-ended questions, but not all open-ended questions elicit higher-order thinking or do so with intent. *Open-ended* describes the form of a question, not the quality of a question. They are simply questions that do not have one correct answer and cannot be answered with a word or two. However, some closed questions can be more compelling and have greater educational value than open-ended questions. Closed questions can require using HOT skills in response and at advanced levels of thinking. The set of questions from the *SnapsHOT* Go with the Flow are closed questions but elicit many HOT skills: "If we had lots of different funnels, which would you choose? How would it be different from this one?" They elicit imagining, associating and differentiating, evaluating, inducing, and more. Here's another example of a closed question that requires advanced levels of multiple HOT skills to answer: "Is this statement from the newspaper an opinion, an opinion presented as a fact, or a fact?" Open-ended questions can be vague and contrived ("What's happening here?" "What's that doing here?"), demeaning and rhetorical ("What's the matter with you?"), or prescriptive and still have only one correct answer or a very limited number of answers ("What is a safe way to cross a street?").

Yet, despite a lack of intentionality, the use of open-ended questions has been widely touted in the field for decades as a superior form of questioning, a key indicator of quality teaching, and a core strategy for scaffolding learning, particularly play-based learning (Haden et al. 2016; Lee and Kinzie 2012; Van de Pol, Volman, and Beishuizen 2010; Weisberg et al. 2016). HOT questions, as a concept, redefine what constitutes a good question by basing the judgment on the quality of the question rather than its form.

Sparks

The purpose of a spark is to get students started on a self-directed line of inquiry or investigation. Sparks take the form of a suggestion, idea, challenge, and/or resource that will engage multiple HOT skills in the course of the inquiry. In the *SnapsHOT* How to Draw a Mirror, on pages 149–150, the teacher suggests that students go into the bathroom to study the properties of mirrors directly.

In the *SnapsHOT* Go with the Flow, on pages 159–160, a student is offered the challenge to change something to stop the water from overfilling the funnel and, a little later, the challenge to investigate the combination of containers, funnels, and pouring techniques that will work best for him. The teacher also makes sure he has the materials to do it.

Why the term *sparks*? Because education is about lighting fires, not filling buckets, as some wise person said. There is even an old expression in the form of a comment to a person deep in thought: "I can smell wood burning."

A second-grade teacher offers a spark to her students during a science unit on the solar system. Although they have seen a computer animation of the planets orbiting the sun, read a short article from a science magazine for children, and watched a demonstration of Earth rotating while orbiting the sun (with a globe and a ball to represent the sun), there has not yet been full and explicit explanations how those events relate to night and day, the length of a year, the seasons, and weather. During one discussion, she tells her students that the sun does not rise and set. After a few students argue with her, she divides the class into three groups, each tasked to either prove that she is wrong or explain why she is right. She provides resources to each group: books, a tablet computer with links to relevant websites, and a flashlight and balls. She gives them a bit of help before they begin: "I said the sun does not rise and set. I did not say there isn't day and night."

The attributes of an effective spark include the following:

- The right kind of information: The teacher gives information that is useful, relevant, understandable, actionable, and likely to lead to a deeper understanding or new knowledge.

- The right timing: The spark is given at an opportune moment when students are ready, motivated, and engaged.

- The right amount of information: The spark gives only as much information as necessary to ensure students can run with it with no or minimal teacher assistance. Spark statements are short and to the point.

- The necessary tools: The teacher provides the necessary materials and supports for students to investigate deeply and thoroughly.

- The offer of assistance: The students know that they can access the teacher and other resources as needed.

- Follow-up: By telling students that there will be a "debriefing," the teacher lets them know their processes, discoveries, insights, and results are important and of high interest to her.

"Heating" an Activity

This is simply the idea of adding an element to a LOT or practical thinking activity that will engage one or more HOT skills. (Yes, it's called "heating" because it makes a typical activity a higher-order thinking [HOT] activity; and, yes, the heat often comes from the fire lit by a "spark!") This can often be done easily and quickly, such as by adding an element of choice, as discussed previously. There are many ways to add creative and critical thinking elements to nearly any activity, which is beneficial to all students and all thinking styles. For example, in addition to practice solving math problems (calculating), students can select one problem and think of the following added elements:

- two different ways to get the answer

- two ways that someone could get the wrong answer

- two other math problems that result in the same answer; for an added challenge, the problems must use two different types of arithmetic, both of which are different from the type used in the problem

- a situation in which they would use it (they could draw a picture, write it, record it, or all three)

- a recipe that incorporates it

- a word problem for it using the characters and setting from a book

Here is another example in the content area of literacy. In addition to reading a story and discussing elements such as plot, theme, sequence of events, characters, and setting, students can

- act out the story;

- create a new character to add to the story;

- think of another plot element that can be inserted into the story;

- think of a different ending;

- place the story in a different time and/or location and make changes to the story accordingly;

- create a sequel or prequel story;

- make up a story that is different but has the same theme.

These activities not only engage higher-order thinking but also help solidify students' understanding of story elements.

Conclusion

The activities described for the teaching techniques in this chapter are examples that should serve as inspiration for activities that will work best for your students. Using one or two of these techniques may have some impact on developing students' HOT skills, but it is the power of their cumulative effect that will have the greatest impact on developing students' higher-order thinking of every type and at the most advanced levels of which they are capable.

Now the apprentice carpenter knows the full range of tools, from the mundane but highly functional hammer to the specialized power and hand tools of the trade. The apprentice knows their purposes and functions, general principles for their use (take good care of them), strategies to apply those principles (check the blade on your miter saw before using it), and techniques for applying the strategies (clean the blade if dirty; to sharpen it, clamp it down and file each tooth with a small diamond file in smooth, upward motions along the edge).

In the same way, teachers now know the full range of thinking skills from the mundane LOT skills like memorizing to powerful HOT skills like parsing false statements presented as facts. They know their purposes and functions. They know principles for using them as teaching tools (activities are challenging and enjoyable), strategies for applying the principles (*ThinkinGames*), and techniques for applying the strategies (offer many choices, ask challenging questions). The certificate of mastery will be signed when promoting the full range of higher-order thinking becomes second nature; when HOT strategies and HOT techniques are infused throughout the curriculum for every subject every day; and when good teaching becomes great teaching because it is HOT teaching.

Key Ideas from This Chapter

HOT techniques give teachers tools to promote higher-order thinking through direct interactions with students. They help teachers implement HOT strategies such as projects, games, and case studies.

Below are some HOT techniques:

- scaffolding with verbal, physical, and material supports

- cues for quickly reminding students to use higher-order thinking

- modeling and demonstrating higher-order thinking regularly and often and making it explicit for young learners

- using figures of speech such as idioms, aphorisms, analogies, and similes to communicate the importance of various types of higher-order thinking

- asking questions that help students think deeply and thoroughly and that challenge them to use many types of higher-order thinking

- offering choices that require students to use higher-order decision-making skills often and regularly

- providing cognitively challenging but meaningful and relevant tasks, called *sparks*, that involve the use of multiple HOT skills

- adding an element to an activity or modifying it slightly to engage higher-order thinking, called "heating" the activity

Questions for Discussion

- In what different ways have you scaffolded students' learning? Share any examples that involved scaffolding their thinking. What thinking skills were promoted? Did the scaffolding sharpen an existing thinking skill or introduce a new one?

- What were some of the common aphorisms you heard as a child and student from parents and teachers? What did they attempt to communicate about thinking? How did they influence your thinking? If you have children, do you repeat the same aphorisms to them? Do you use new ones?

- How have you modeled behaviors or thinking skills or processes for students? How did you promote transferring the behaviors or thinking skills and avoid imitation?

- Are there other techniques that you have used or that you think could be used to promote HOT skills that were not covered in this chapter?

Teaching Reading and Writing Using Higher-Order Thinking:
Yearning to Learn

Is it possible to teach complex cognitive and technical skills like reading, or complex cognitive and mechanical skills like writing, with higher-order thinking? After all, practicing to write the letter *e* is necessary and is a motor task for which higher-order thinking is irrelevant. And tasks like learning to recognize and know the sounds of blends or memorizing sight words are necessary to learn to read but only require LOT skills. Learning to read takes lots of practice and effort. It involves struggling with long and unfamiliar words, losing and finding one's place in the text, and other not-so-fun tasks. On the road to reading, there is no avoiding those mundane, repetitive, joyless, drill-and-practice tolls and pit stops. The road is a lot more LOT than HOT!

Agreed. These are the very reasons why everything about learning to read that can possibly involve critical and creative thinking needs to involve critical and creative thinking. If we do this, the bumps, tolls, and pit stops will be minor inconveniences on an enjoyable journey full of adventures. Of all the things that can and should involve HOT skills, one of the most important and impactful is the quality of the texts with which students learn to read. It is as important as any

HOT teaching strategy or technique to ensure that students work with materials developed by adults who used higher-order thinking skills to create them. Inauthentic texts, commonly found in commercial reading curricula, sacrifice meaning for some notion of instructional value, which is another way of saying they engage LOT skills at the expense of HOT skills. They are not benign. They stifle students' motivation to want to read. Quality texts, on the other hand, can engage LOT, MOT, and HOT skills and motivate students to want to read. With so much great children's literature available, both classic and contemporary, it is also difficult to justify not using high-quality authentic texts. Quality texts are not only for students to read for themselves or to teachers, but for teachers to read to students. At every grade level, students need to hear wonderful stories read to them from books that are several reading levels more advanced than their own.

There are many great children's books, but here are the ones mentioned in this book that meet the definition of quality: *Lilly's Purple Plastic Purse* (Henkes 2006a), *Where the Wild Things Are* (Sendak 1963), *The Lion and the Mouse* (Pinkney 2009), *No, David!* (Shannon 1998), *Swimmy* (Lionni [1963] 2013), *Frederick* (Lionni 1967), *A Color of His Own* (Lionni [1975] 2006), *An Apple for Harriet Tubman* (Turner 2016), *Horton Hatches the Egg* (Seuss [1940] 2013), and *Horton Hears a Who!* ([1954] 2013). These authors' deep understanding of children's emotional and cognitive needs, concerns, and interests reflect their advanced critical thinking skills. But it is their advanced creative thinking skills that enable them to use this understanding to create stories that children can comprehend, connect to, and delight in.

Throughout the book, I have described many literacy activities in which students both develop and practice higher-order thinking. Using some logical thinking, I have categorized them by their main characteristics. And using some creative thinking, I have added a few new activities.

Writing That Is Meaningful and Learner Centered

Scaffolded writing is discussed in the section about representational thinking on page 148. Developed by Bodrova and Leong (2007), scaffolded writing is a literacy development strategy in which preliterate children use lines to represent words to "write" meaningful and purposeful messages. This is also a tool that teachers can use as a bridge to conventional writing.

Students write their own stories and make their own books. The books students make should engage one or more HOT skills or processes. The books need to be intentional by having a purpose and a defined audience, such as a message to parents or to "my future self." They can also reflect or complement the style or genre of a recently read story. For example, after reading *Horton Hatches the Egg* and *Horton Hears a Who!*, second- and third-grade students can research whether elephants actually are faithful, empathetic, and protective and write books about the social traits of elephants. Then they can write fantasy books about elephants' other social traits using the style of Dr. Seuss or the character of Horton.

Another type of book students can write are guidebooks, which entail critical reflection (a type of critical analysis). Near the end of the school year, third graders create a *Survival Guide* for current second graders to help them be successful in third grade. Second graders can do the same for first graders, first graders for kindergartners, and kindergartners for preschoolers.

Author and Theme Studies

A study that is both an author and theme study is described on page 119. The theme is Me and We, and the author is Leo Lionni. His books are about the many ways that an individual can have a unique identity but still be vital member of a group. *Frederick* the mouse finds his role in the mouse community as a storyteller and poet. *Swimmy* is the only black fish among his red schoolmates. But when they swim together in the formation of a large fish to scare off predators, his unique color makes for the perfect eye. Other common themes found in children's literature are friendship in the Frog and Toad series by Arnold Lobel; parents' unconditional love for their children in the David books by David Shannon and in many of Maurice Sendak's books; and the sometimes up-and-down relationships between students and teachers in the Ramona books by Beverly Cleary, the Miss Nelson books by Harry Allard, and the Lilly books by Kevin Henkes.

Word Games

Rhyme Time, on page 116: guessing rhyming words from pictures or actions

Don't Say the Word!, on page 136: guessing an object or idea from its description

Chain Stories, on page 138: everyone contributes sequentially to spontaneously making up a story

Analogies and Expressions

The literature-based analogies and expressions from chapter 9 on page 157 include "You are kinder than the lion who didn't eat the mouse!" "You two are the best friends since Frog met Toad!" "I got dirtier than Harry on a bad day!" "This room looks like David and Curious George had a party!" "How old am I? If I were a turtle, I'd be more Morla than Mutant Ninja." Here is another that plays off the theme in *Lilly's Big Day* (Henkes 2006b). It describes wishful thinking as "The flower girl at Mr. Slinger's wedding" or an action as "Throwing flowers at Mr. Slinger's wedding." It is a combination of "Don't count your chickens before they hatch" and "Building castles in the sky." Given some prompts, students can create expressions based on the personalities and actions of characters in the books they read: "This is funnier than (character) (action or situation)." "You are as clever as (character) (action or situation)."

Heating a Literacy Activity

Ideas for adding an element of creativity to discussions of books and stories from page 164 include acting out the story, creating a new character for the story, thinking of another plot element that can be inserted into the story, thinking of a different ending to the story, rewriting the story to place it in a different time and/or location, creating a sequel or prequel story, and making up a story that is different but has the same theme.

Supporting Every Unique Reader

Learning to read requires a great deal of time practicing. My experience with my own three children, and with the many children I have worked with, is that every child has her own unique approach to learning to read, regardless of instructional method. It's like teaching handwriting—no matter which style you teach or how you teach it, every person's handwriting will be different. A key to learning to read is to spend many hours reading aloud with an attentive adult who judiciously offers individualized assistance, corrections, and suggestions for reading strategies; who helps keep the focus on the meaning and the enjoyment of the story; and who, most of all, gives copious amounts of encouragement. For my oldest son, who was mostly a phonetic reader, I helped him learn to also use contextual cues and to focus more on meaning. For my contextual-reading daughter and youngest child, I encouraged her to slow down and sound out a word occasionally. For my middle son who used both in equal measure, I helped him strengthen both, but mostly I just tried to be a patient and appreciative listener. It may be that the best reading "curriculum" is to give parents, community members, retired friends and relatives, office staff, high school students, volunteers, and others training and support to guide children as they read aloud.

The following poetic saying, which is not a direct quote but has been paraphrased from the writings of Antoine de Saint-Exupéry (2003), expresses my beliefs about teaching reading:

> If you want to build a ship, don't drum up the men to gather wood, divide the work, and give orders. Instead, teach them to yearn for the vast and endless sea.

This saying is not meant to be taken literally, but it makes an important point about the value of intrinsic motivation. This is also true of my version:

> If you want to teach children to read, don't make them decode nonsense. Instead, teach them to yearn for a place where wild things roar and sidewalks end, but stories never do.

Appendix:
Activities Cross-Referenced by Content Area

	Art	Music/Drama	Language and Literacy	Natural Science
SnapsHOTs				
"Cheetahed"?, p. 96				Animal traits
Drought, p. 36				Climate, drought, ecology
Float Your Boat, p. 65	Design, create			
Free the Trees!, p. 29			Writing, research	Botany, ecology
Go with the Flow, p. 159			Science vocabulary, articulation	
Harriet 'Round the Mountain, p. 112		Song: "She'll Be Coming 'Round the Mountain"; song origins	Book: *An Apple for Harriet Tubman*	
How to Draw a Mirror, p. 149	Drawing to represent reflection			
Is the Sky Falling? p. 105			Story of Henny Penny	
It's Time to Party, p. 69				
Lilly, p. 35	Graphical representations of concepts		Book: *Lilly's Purple Plastic Purse*; plot devices.	
Lincoln Thinkin', p. 97			Biography	

	Physical Science	Math	History/Culture	Social/Emotional
SnapsHOTs				
"Cheetahed"?, p. 96				
Drought, p. 36				
Float Your Boat, p. 65	Flotation	Collect/analyze data		
Free the Treesl, p. 29			Urban community	Control
Go with the Flow, p. 159	Properties of water			
Harriet 'Round the Mountain, p. 112			Slavery, Underground Railroad	Empathy, compassion
How to Draw a Mirror, p. 149	Mirrors, reflective materials			
Is the Sky Falling? p. 105				
It's Time to Party, p. 69				
Lilly, p. 35				
Lincoln Thinkin', p. 97			Abe Lincoln	Trust

	Art	Music/Drama	Language and Literacy	Natural Science
SnapsHOTs				
Orange Is the New Green, p. 146				
Reframing a Parent/School Conflict, p. 68				
Questions for an Author, p. 48	Artist working in her studio		Reading books by the same author, writing process	
A Special Lunch, p. 107				
Why It's Hard to Explain Why, p. 82			Vocabulary to describe feelings	
Wild and Tame, p. 119		Acting out stories	Inventing stories	Large cats, animal habitats, concepts of wildness/ tameness
Cognitivities				
Brain Baits, p. 95	Can be adapted for any content area			
The Case of the Unknown Bully, p. 139			Mystery story	
Inventors Inventing Inventions, p. 59	Can be adapted for any content area			
Making Maps, p. 51	Symbols represent objects; aerial perspective			
May the Best Map Win, p. 77				
Same Words, Different Meanings, p. 53			Inferring meaning from speech patterns	

	Physical Science	Math	History/Culture	Social/Emotional
SnapsHOTs				
Orange Is the New Green, p. 146	Oxidation of metal; gears, simple machines			Preferences, biases
Reframing a Parent/School Conflict, p. 68				
Questions for an Author, p. 48				
A Special Lunch, p. 107		Sets, graphing, weighting, calculating	Culture-based food preferences	Cultural pride
Why It's Hard to Explain Why, p. 82				Expressing feelings
Wild and Tame, p. 119				Impulse-control, strong emotions
Cognitivities				
Brain Baits, p. 95	Can be adapted for any content area			
The Case of the Unknown Bully, p. 139				Social relationships, anti-bullying
Inventors Inventing Inventions, p. 59	Can be adapted for any content area			
Making Maps, p. 51		Representing narrative criteria with numbers		
May the Best Map Win, p. 77			Participation in democratic process	Fairness, appreciation of others' abilities
Same Words, Different Meanings, p. 53				

	Art	Music/Drama	Language and Literacy	Natural Science
ThinkinGames				
The Art of Lotto, p. 26	Paintings, artists, genres, media	Lotto cards can be made to reflect any content area.		
Chain Stories, p. 138			Elements of stories such as plot, character, setting	
Conductor, p. 39		Music directions		
Describe It/ Draw It, p. 137	Drawing		Communicate clearly and accurately	
Don't Say the Word!, p. 136			Vocabulary	
Family Groups, p. 62	Can be adapted for any content area			
Game of Stones, p. 40	Color nuances			Qualities of stones
Rhyme Time, p. 116	Can be adapted for any content area			
Shape Shifting, p. 58			Descriptive vocabulary	
Twins, p. 134				
HOT Themes				
Brain Power, p. 118			Roald Dahl's books; fairy tales: "Puss in Boots" and "Tom Thumb"	
Good, Better, Best, p. 118				
Luck Doesn't Last, p. 118				
Me and We, p. 119			Leo Lionni's books	
No Fair!, p. 118				
Winning and Losing, p. 118				

	Physical Science	Math	History/Culture	Social/Emotional
ThinkinGames				
The Art of Lotto, p. 26	Lotto cards can be made to reflect any content area.			
Chain Stories, p. 138				Collaboration
Conductor, p. 39				
Describe It/Draw It, p. 137	Drawing		Communicate clearly and accurately	
Don't Say the Word!, p. 136			Vocabulary	
Family Groups, p. 62	Can be adapted for any content area			
Game of Stones, p. 40				
Rhyme Time, p. 116	Can be adapted for any content area			
Shape Shifting, p. 58			Descriptive vocabulary	
Twins, p. 134				
HOT Themes				
Brain Power, p. 118			Justice, brains over brawn	Feeling powerful
Good, Better, Best, p. 118			Fair evaluation, collegiality	Ability differences; appreciation of others' abilities
Luck Doesn't Last, p. 118		Chance, odds		
Me and We, p. 119			Contributing to the community	Self-efficacy
No Fair!, p. 118			Social justice, equity, equality	Fairness
Winning and Losing, p. 118				Feelings about losing, being a gracious winner

References

Abrami, Philip C., Robert M. Bernard, Eugene Borokhovski, David I. Waddington, C. Anne Wade, and Tonje Persson. 2015. "Strategies for Teaching Students to Think Critically: A Meta-analysis." *Review of Educational Research* 85 (2): 275–314.

Bloom, B. S., M. D. Engelhart, E. J. Furst, W. H. Hill, and D. R. Krathwohl. 1956. *Taxonomy of Educational Objectives: The Categorization of Educational Goals. Handbook I: Cognitive Domain.* New York: David McKay Company.

Bodrova, Elena, and Deborah J. Leong. 2007. *Tools of the Mind: The Vygotskian Approach to Early Childhood Education.* 2nd ed. Upper Saddle River, NJ: Pearson Education.

Bonawitz, E. B., P. Shafto, H. Gweon, N. D. Goodman, E. S. Spelke, and L. Schulz. 2011. "The Double-Edged Sword of Pedagogy: Instruction Limits Spontaneous Exploration and Discovery." *Cognition* 120 (3): 322–30.

Brannon, E. M., and J. Park, eds. 2015. "Phylogeny and Ontogeny of Mathematical and Numerical Understanding." In *Oxford Handbook of Numerical Cognition,* edited by Roi Cohen Kadosh and Ann Dowker, 203–13. Oxford: Oxford University Press.

Buchsbaum, D., A. Gopnik, T. L. Griffiths, and P. Shafto. 2011. "Children's Imitation of Causal Action Sequences Is Influenced by Statistical and Pedagogical Evidence." *Cognition* 120 (3): 331–40.

Burgoyne, Alexander P., Giovanni Sala, Fernand Gobet, Brooke N. Macnamara, Guillermo Campitelli, and David Z. Hambrick. 2016. "The Relationship between Cognitive Ability and Chess Skill: A Comprehensive Meta-analysis." *Intelligence* 59 (2016): 72–83.

Celli, Lynne M., and Nicholas D. Young. 2014. *Learning Style Perspectives: Impact in the Classroom.* Madison, WI: Atwood Publishing.

Center for Public Education. 2007. "What Research Says about the Value of Homework: Research Review." Center for Public Education. www.centerforpubliceducation.org/research/what-research-says-about-value-homework-research-review.

Chomsky, Noam. 1965. *Aspects of the Theory of Syntax*. Cambridge, MA: MIT Press.

Cimpian, A., and E. Salomon. 2014. "The Inherence Heuristic: An Intuitive Means of Making Sense of the World, and a Potential Precursor to Psychological Essentialism." *Behavioral and Brain Sciences* 37:461–480.

Clements, Douglas H., and Julie Sarama. 2014. "Play, Mathematics, and False Dichotomies." *Preschool Matters Today* (blog). National Institute for Early Education Research. March 3. http://nieer.org/2014/03/03/play-mathematics-and-false-dichotomies

Collins, Robyn. 2014. "Skills for the 21st Century: Teaching Higher-Order Thinking." *Curriculum & Leadership Journal* 12 (14). www.curriculum.edu.au/leader/teaching_higher_order_thinking,37431.html?issueID=12910.

Covington, Martin. V., Richard R. Crutchfield, Lillian B. Davies, and Robert M. Olton. 1972. *The Productive Thinking Program*. Columbus, OH: Merrill.

Daly, Lisa, and Miriam Beloglovsky. 2014. *Loose Parts: Inspiring Play in Young Children*. St. Paul, MN: Redleaf Press.

de Bono, Edward. 1985. "The Practical Teaching of Thinking Using the CoRT Method." *Special Services in the Schools* 3 (1–2): 33–47.

Dehaene, S. 2011. *Number Sense: How the Mind Creates Mathematics*. Rev. ed. Oxford: Oxford University Press.

Dyer, Frank, and Thomas Martin. 1910. *Edison: His Life and Inventions. Vol. 2*. New York: Harper & Brothers.

Elango, Sneha, Jorge Luis García, James J. Heckman, and Andrés Hojman. 2016. "Early Childhood Education." In *Economics of Means-Tested Transfer Programs in the United States, Volume 2*, edited by Robert. A. Moffitt , 235–97. Chicago: University of Chicago Press.

Feigenson, Lisa, Stanislas Dehaene, and Elizabeth Spelke. 2004. "Core Systems of Number." *Trends in Cognitive Sciences* 8 (7): 307–314.

Feuerstein, Reuven, Refael S. Feuerstein, and Louis H. Falik. 2010. *Beyond Smarter: Mediated Learning and the Brain's Capacity to Change.* New York: Teachers College Press.

Food Marketing Institute. 2016. *U.S. Grocery Shopper Trends 2016.* Arlington, VA: Food Marketing Institute.

Gardner, Howard. 2011. *Frames of Mind: The Theory of Multiple Intelligences.* 3rd ed. New York: Basic Books.

Goodwin, Bryan. 2017. "Research Matters / Critical Thinking Won't Develop through Osmosis." *Educational Leadership* 74 (5): 80–81.

Gopnik, Alison. 2016a. *The Gardener and the Carpenter: What the New Science of Child Development Tells Us about the Relationship between Parents and Children.* New York: Farrar, Straus and Giroux.

———. 2016b. "What Babies Know about Physics and Foreign Languages." *New York Times Sunday Review: Opinion.* July 30. www.nytimes.com/2016/07/31/opinion/sunday/what-babies-know-about-physics-and-foreign-languages.html.

Greene, Joshua. 2013. *Moral Tribes: Emotion, Reason, and the Gap between Us and Them.* New York: Penguin Press.

Haden, C. A., T. Cohen, D. Uttal, and M. Marcus. 2016. "Building Learning: Narrating Experiences in a Children's Museum." In *Cognitive Development in Museum Settings: Relating Research and Practice,* edited by D. M. Sobel and J. L. Jipson, 84–103. New York: Routledge.

Halpern, Diane F. 2012. *Sex Differences in Cognitive Abilities.* 4th ed. Hove, UK: Psychology Press.

Hamlin, J. K., G. E. Newman, and K. Wynn. 2009. "Eight-Month-Old Infants Infer Unfulfilled Goals, Despite Ambiguous Physical Evidence." *Infancy* 14 (5): 579–90.

Hamlin, J. K., and K. Wynn. 2011. "Young Infants Prefer Prosocial to Antisocial Others." *Cognitive Development* 26 (1): 30–39.

Hamlin, J. K., K. Wynn, and P. Bloom. 2007. "Social Evaluation by Preverbal Infants." *Nature* 450 (7169): 557–59.

———. 2010. "Three-Month-Olds Show a Negativity Bias in Their Social Evaluations." *Developmental Science* 13 (6): 923–29.

Henkes, Kevin. 2006a. *Lilly's Purple Plastic Purse.* New York: Greenwillow Books.

———. 2006b. *Lilly's Big Day.* New York: Greenwillow Books.

Higgins, S., E. Hall, V. Baumfield, and D. Moseley. 2005. "A Meta analysis of the Impact of the Implementation of Thinking Skills Approaches on Pupils." *Research in Education Library* (October). London: EPPI-Centre, Social Science Research. https://eppi.ioe.ac.uk/cms/LinkClick.aspx?fileticket=ejoc10d5sWY%3D&tabid=339&mid=1262.

Hines, M. 2010. "Sex-Related Variation in Human Behavior and the Brain." *Trends in Cognitive Sciences* 14 (10): 448–56.

Hirsh-Pasek, Kathy, Roberta Michnick Golinkoff, Laura E. Berk, and Dorothy G. Singer. 2009. *A Mandate for Playful Learning in Preschool: Presenting the Evidence.* New York: Oxford University Press.

Hofstede, Geert. 2011. "Dimensionalizing Cultures: The Hofstede Model in Context." *Online Readings in Psychology and Culture* 2 (1). https://doi.org/10.9707/2307-0919.1014.

Inhelder, B., and Jean Piaget. 1958. *The Growth of Logical Thinking from Childhood to Adolescence: An Essay on the Construction of Formal Operational Structures.* New York: Basic Books.

Kahneman, Daniel. 2011. *Thinking, Fast and Slow.* New York: Farrar, Straus and Giroux.

Katz, Lilian. 2015. *Lively Minds: Distinctions between Academic versus Intellectual Goals for Young Children.* Washington, DC: Defending the Early Years. https://deyproject.files.wordpress.com/2015/04/dey-lively-minds-4-8-15.pdf.

Krathwohl, David R. 2002. "A Revision of Bloom's Taxonomy: An Overview." *Theory into Practice* 41 (4): 212–18.

Lee, Youngju, and Mable B. Kinzie. 2012. "Teacher Question and Student Response with Regard to Cognition and Language Use." *Instructional Science* 40:857–74.

Leong, Deborah J., and Elena Bodrova. 2012. "Assessing and Scaffolding: Make-Believe Play." *Young Children* 67 (1): 28–34.

Lewis, Katherine Reynolds. 2016. "Abandon Parenting, and Just Be a Parent." *Atlantic*. September 23. www.theatlantic.com/education/archive/2016/09 /abandon-parenting-and-just-be-a-parent/501236.

Lionni, Leo. (1963) 2013. *Swimmy*. 50th Anniversary edition. New York: Knopf Books for Young Readers.

———. 1967. *Frederick*. New York: Random House.

———. (1975) 2006. *A Color of His Own*. New York: Knopf Books for Young Readers.

Lun, Vivian Miu-Chi. 2010. "Examining the Influence of Culture on Critical Thinking in Higher Education." PhD diss., Victoria University of Wellington, NZ. http://researcharchive.vuw.ac.nz/handle/10063/1211.

Mahajan, Neha, and Karen Wynn. 2012. "Origins of 'Us' versus 'Them': Prelinguistic Infants Prefer Similar Others." *Cognition* 124 (2): 227–33.

Maslow, Abraham H. 1966. *The Psychology of Science: A Reconnaissance*. New York: Harper & Row.

Merriam-Webster. 2003. *Merriam-Webster's Collegiate Dictionary*. 11th ed. Springfield, MA: Merriam-Webster.

Mischel, Walter, Ebbe B. Ebbesen, and Antonette Raskoff Zeiss. 1972. "Cognitive and Attentional Mechanisms in Delay of Gratification." *Journal of Personality and Social Psychology* 21 (2): 204–18.

National Center for Education Statistics. 2016. *The Nation's Report Card 2015*. Washington, DC: National Center for Education Statistics, Institute of Education Sciences, US Department of Education.

Noguera, Pedro, Linda Darling-Hammond, and Diane Friedlaender. 2015. "Equal Opportunity for Deeper Learning." Jobs for the Future. www.jff.org/publications/equal-opportunity-deeper-learning.

Pianta, Robert C., Jay Belsky, Renate Houts, and Fred Morrison. 2007. "Opportunities to Learn in America's Elementary Classrooms." *Science* 315 (5820): 1795–96.

Pinkney, Jerry. 2009. *The Lion and the Mouse*. New York: Little, Brown.

Pinker, S., and E. Spelke. 2005. *The Science of Gender and Science: Pinker vs. Spelke, a Debate*. Presented at the Mind Brain Behavior Interfaculty Initiative (MBB), Harvard University, April 22. http://edge.org/3rd_culture/debate05/debate05_index.html.

Pritchard, Alan. 2017. *Ways of Learning: Learning Theories for the Classroom*. 4th ed. London: Routledge.

Rayner, S., and E. Cools, eds. 2011. *Style Differences in Cognition, Learning, and Management: Theory, Research, and Practice*. New York: Taylor & Francis Group.

Robson, Sue. 2012. *Developing Thinking and Understanding in Young Children: An Introduction for Students*. Abingdon, UK: Routledge.

Saifer, Steffen. 2010. "Higher Order Play and Its Role in Development and Education." *Psychological Science and Education Journal of the Moscow State University* 3:38–50.

———. 2017. *Practical Solutions to Practically Every Problem: The Survival Guide for Early Childhood Professionals*. 3rd ed. St. Paul, MN: Redleaf Press.

Saifer, Steffen, Keisha Edwards, Debbie Ellis, Lena Ko, and Amy Stuczynski. 2011. *Culturally Responsive Standards-Based Teaching: Classroom to Community and Back*. 2nd ed. Thousand Oaks, CA: Corwin Press.

Saint-Exupéry, Antoine de. 2003. *Wisdom of the Sands*. Mattituck, NY: Amereon Press.

Sala, Giovanni, and Fernando Gobet. 2016. "Do the Benefits of Chess Instruction Transfer to Academic and Cognitive Skills? A Meta-analysis." *Educational Research Review* 18 (May 2016): 46–57.

Saracho, Olivia, ed. 2017. *Cognitive Style in Early Education*. London: Routledge.

Scott-Weich, Bridget, and David B. Yaden Jr. 2017. "Scaffolded Writing and Early Literacy Development with Children Who Are Deaf: A Case Study." *Early Child Development and Care* 187 (3–4): 418–35.

Sendak, Maurice. 1963. *Where the Wild Things Are*. New York: Harper & Row.

Seuss, Dr. (1940) 2013. *Horton Hatches the Egg*. New York: Random House.

———. (1954) 2013. *Horton Hears a Who!* New York: Random House.

Shannon, David. 1998. *No, David!* New York: Blue Sky Press.

Siegler, R. S., and M. W. Alibali. 2005. *Children's Thinking*. 4th ed. New York: Pearson.

Sternberg, Robert J. 1988. "Mental Self-Government: A Theory of Intellectual Styles and Their Development." *Human Development* 31 (4): 197–224.

Sternberg, Robert J., Elena Grigorenko, and Li-Fang Zhang. 2008. "Styles of Learning and Thinking Matter in Instruction and Assessment." *Perspectives on Psychological Science* 3 (6): 486–506.

Swartz, Robert J., Arthur L. Costa, Barry K. Beyer, Rebecca Reagan, and Bena Kallick. 2010. *Thinking-Based Learning: Promoting Quality Student Achievement in the 21st Century.* New York: Teachers College Press.

Taylor, L. E., A. L. Swerdfeger, and G. D. Eslick. 2014. "Vaccines Are Not Associated with Autism: An Evidence-Based Meta-analysis of Case-Control and Cohort Studies." *Vaccine* 32 (29): 3623–29.

Thomson, Derek. 2015. "Lotteries: America's $70 Billion Shame." *Atlantic.* May 11. www.theatlantic.com/business/archive/2015/05/lotteries-americas-70-billion-shame/392870/.

Touhill, Luke. 2012. "How to Draw a Mirror." *National Quality Standard Professional Learning Program e-Newsletter* 43:3. Deakin West, Australia: Early Childhood Australia. www.earlychildhoodaustralia.org.au/nqsplp/wp-content/uploads/2012/09/NQS_PLP_E-Newsletter_No43.pdf.

Turner, Glennette Tilley. 2016. *An Apple for Harriet Tubman.* Park Ridge, IL: Albert Whitman.

Van de Pol, Janneke, Monique Volman, and Jos Beishuizen. 2010. "Scaffolding in Teacher-Student Interaction: A Decade of Research." *Educational Psychology Review* 22 (3): 271–96.

Viereck, George Sylvester. 1929. "What Life Means to Einstein: An Interview by George Sylvester Viereck." *Saturday Evening Post* October 26.

Vygotsky, Lev. 1978. "The Role of Play in Development." In *Mind in Society* by Lev Vygotsky, 92–104. Cambridge, MA: Harvard University Press.

Weiland, Christina, and Hirokazu Yoshikawa. 2013. "Impacts of a Prekindergarten Program on Children's Mathematics, Language, Literacy, Executive Function, and Emotional Skills." *Child Development* 84 (6): 2112–30.

Weisberg, Deena Skolnick, Kathy Hirsh-Pasek, and Roberta Michnick Golinkoff. 2013. "Guided Play: Where Curricular Goals Meet a Playful Pedagogy." *Mind, Brain, and Education* 7 (2): 104–12. www.sas.upenn.edu/~deenas/papers/weisberg-hirshpasek-golinkoff-mbe-2013.pdf.

Weisberg, Deena Skolnick, Kathy Hirsh-Pasek, Roberta Michnick Golinkoff, Audrey K. Kittredge, and David Klahr. 2016. "Guided Play: Principles and Practices." *Current Directions in Psychological Science* 25 (3): 177–82. http://journals.sagepub.com/doi/pdf/10.1177/0963721416645512.

Willingham, Daniel T. 2007. "Critical Thinking: Why Is It So Hard to Teach?" *American Educator* (Summer): 8–19.

Wineburg, Sam, Sarah McGrew, Joel Breakstone, and Teresa Ortega. 2016. *Evaluating Information: The Cornerstone of Civic Online Reasoning.* Stanford History Education Group: Stanford, CA. https://stacks.stanford.edu/file/druid:fv751yt5934/SHEG%20Evaluating%20Information%20Online.pdf.

Witkin, H. A., R. B. Dyk, H. F. Faterson, D. R. Goodenough, and S. A. Karp. 1962. *Psychological Differentiation.* New York: John Wiley & Sons.

Zhang, Li-Fang, and Robert Sternberg. 2005. "A Threefold Model of Intellectual Styles." *Educational Psychology Review* 17 (1): 1–53.

Zhang, Li-Fang, Robert Sternberg, and Stephen Rayner, eds. 2012. *Handbook of Intellectual Styles Preferences in Cognition, Learning, and Thinking.* New York: Springer.

Index